THE VICTORY OF JESUS

A DEVOTIONAL CELEBRATING EASTER, THE
ASCENSION, AND PENTECOST

HOLIDAY CELEBRATION DEVOTIONALS
BOOK 3

PETER DEHAAN

The Victory of Jesus: A Devotional Celebrating Easter, the Ascension, and Pentecost

Copyright © 2023 by Peter DeHaan.

Book 3 in the Holiday Celebration Devotionals Series.

All Scripture quotations, unless otherwise indicated, are taken from the Holy Bible, New International Version®, NIV®. Copyright © 1973, 1978, 1984, 2011 by Biblica, Inc. ™ Used by permission of Zondervan. All rights reserved worldwide. www.zondervan.com The "NIV" and "New International Version" are trademarks registered in the United States Patent and Trademark Office by Biblica, Inc.™

Library of Congress Control Number: 9798888090367

Published by Rock Rooster Books, Grand Rapids, Michigan

ISBNs:

- 979-8-88809-035-0 (e-book)
- 979-8-88809-036-7 (paperback)
- 979-8-88809-037-4 (hardcover)
- 979-8-88809-038-1 (audiobook)

Credits:

- Developmental editor: Julie Harbison
- Copyeditor: Robyn Mulder
- Cover design: Taryn Nergaard
- Author photo: Chelsie Jensen Photography

To Paulette Freeman

Series by Peter DeHaan

Holiday Celebration Devotionals rejoice in the holidays with Jesus.

40-Day Bible Study Series takes a fresh and practical look into Scripture, book by book.

Bible Character Sketches Series celebrates people in Scripture, from the well-known to the obscure.

Visiting Churches Series takes an in-person look at church practices and traditions to inform and inspire today's followers of Jesus.

Be the first to hear about Peter's new books and receive updates at PeterDeHaan.com/updates.

CONTENTS

CELEBRATING THE VICTORY OF JESUS

Most Christians and churches celebrate the season of Easter, which on many church calendars starts on Easter Sunday (Resurrection Sunday) and lasts fifty days to Pentecost. Some call this season Eastertide.

During this time, we remember Jesus's resurrection from the grave (Easter Sunday); forty days later, his return to heaven (Ascension Day); and ten days after that, the Holy Spirit filling Jesus's followers (Pentecost). In this devotional, we'll celebrate all three as we look at the biblical story that spans these fifty days.

Some people praise Jesus as the suffering Savior and others applaud him as the risen Savior. He is, of course, both our suffering Savior *and* our risen Savior.

Jesus suffered and died for all the wrong things we have done—and will do. In doing so, he serves as the ultimate sin sacrifice to end all sin sacrifices.

When Jesus rises from the grave, he proves he has mastery over death. He no longer needs to die, and we no longer need any more sin sacrifices. He died once to save all people, throughout all time, for all their shortcomings. In doing so, he makes us right with Father God.

His resurrection confirms the finality of what he did.

His resurrection also marks a new covenant between God and us. It replaces the prior covenant instituted in the Old Testament. By dying and rising from the dead, Jesus is victorious. He changes everything.

This book celebrates his glorious victory. It begins with him rising from the dead, then his return to heaven to intercede for us, and later the arrival of the Holy Spirit to guide us and remind us of all Jesus said and did.

We'll open our remembrance with a recap of his sacrificial death on the cross for our sins

(Prologue) and move directly into his resurrection on Easter Sunday (Day 1).

Yet much happens between his death and resurrection, so we'll spend six days looking back at these events (Day 2 through Day 7). Then, starting on Day 8, we'll cover what happens after he rises from the dead, marking his return to heaven on Day 40 and the Holy Spirit's arrival on Day 50.

Along the way, we'll incorporate Old Testament prophecy to expand our understanding of what Jesus did. As we do, we'll also tap our imagination to better see things from the perspective of Jesus and his followers.

The Bible records this in the four biographies of Jesus—Matthew, Mark, Luke, and John—as well as in the book of Acts. Since the apostle John gives us the most content for these events in his narrative, we'll focus on his account and weave in the other authors' passages as needed. After that, we'll switch our attention to the book of Acts to complete our exploration.

May God speak to you during this Easter season.

PROLOGUE: THE DEATH OF JESUS

TODAY'S PASSAGE: JOHN 19:28–30, WITH
MATTHEW 27:45–54, MARK 15:33–39, AND
LUKE 23:44–48

Focus verse: *Jesus said, "It is finished." With that, he bowed his head and gave up his spirit.* (John 19:30)

Together, Matthew, Mark, Luke, and John combine to record seven things Jesus says on the cross as he dies.

One of them is, "My God, why have you forsaken me?" At this moment, Father God has turned his back on Jesus so his Son can complete his mission on his own. This is as it must be.

His last words are, "It is finished." With that, Jesus drops his head and surrenders his will to live, releasing his Spirit.

Jesus is dead.

He dies in our place on the cross, serving as the ultimate sin sacrifice to end all sin sacrifices. In doing so, he fulfills what he came to do and what he told his disciples would happen—on three separate occasions.

At the time of his death, three things occur.

First, the curtain in the temple rips from top to bottom. This suggests that God starts the split from above, something no person could do while standing on the ground. This symbolizes that through Jesus's death all people can now enter the holy of holies and approach God directly. They no longer need a priest to serve as their intermediary.

Next, an earthquake occurs, and tombs break open. The bodies of many holy people rise to life. We don't know who they are or how many, only that they lived holy lives. Were they martyred for their faith? Did they live in faithful expectation of Jesus? How long had they been dead?

Third, the centurion, who sees what happens— along with the guards standing watch—says, "Surely, he was a righteous man." What a profound testimony. And it comes from a non-Jew, a nonbeliever.

We can hope the experience forever changed the centurion, just as it can forever change us.

Questions: *What do you think about the things that happened when Jesus died? Which of the details of Jesus's death most affects you?*

Prayer: Jesus, thank you for loving us so much that you died in our place for our sins to make us right with Father God and allowing us to spend eternity in heaven.

DAY 1: EASTER SUNDAY: HE HAS RISEN!

TODAY'S PASSAGE: JOHN 20:1–18

Focus verse: *Mary Magdalene went to the disciples with the news: "I have seen the Lord!"* (John 20:18)

J esus dies. His body is prepared for burial and his human shell is placed in a tomb. A large stone seals the entrance.

But this isn't the end. In many respects, it's the beginning. Three days later, he rises from the dead. Here's what happens:

After his death, Jesus's body is laid hastily in the tomb before the start of the Sabbath. With the Sabbath now over, Mary Magdalene heads to the tomb early the next morning, while it's still dark. When she arrives, she's shocked at what she sees.

The stone that blocked access to his tomb is no longer there. This isn't what she expected.

She runs to tell Peter and John (the disciple Jesus loved) what she assumes happened: "They've taken Jesus's body from the tomb, and I don't know where they put him."

Peter and John run to Jesus's grave. John gets there first and peers inside. When Peter arrives, he goes right in. The burial cloths are there, but Jesus's body is gone. Seeing for themselves, they believe what Mary said—that his body is gone—and they leave.

Mary, however, stays at the tomb, tears flowing. She sees two angels inside. They ask her why she's crying. "They've taken my Lord away, and I don't know where they moved him."

Jesus—now very much alive—walks up behind her. "Why are you crying?"

She assumes he's the gardener and asks where he moved the body.

Jesus calls her by name. "Mary."

She turns to him and cries out in relief.

Jesus tells her to go and tell the disciples he's alive and will soon return to his Father in heaven. In doing so, Jesus tasks Mary to deliver the most important message throughout all history. "Jesus is alive! He's risen from the dead!"

Though her culture doesn't accept a woman's testimony, Jesus doesn't care. Mary will serve fine as his messenger.

This makes her the first missionary to tell others the good news about Jesus.

We call this day Easter when we celebrate his resurrection from the tomb. A better label is Resurrection Sunday.

On this first Resurrection Sunday, Jesus is victorious over the finality of death. This proves his mastery over the grave. Through this resurrection power he provides, we, too, can rise from the dead. And if we follow Jesus, we will.

Then we'll live with him and Father God forever.

Questions: *What can we do to celebrate what Jesus did when he died and rose again? How can we best tell others about him?*

Prayer: Jesus, may we celebrate your victory over

death when you rose from the dead. May we tell others the good news.

DAY 2: THE WOMEN AT THE CROSS

TODAY'S PASSAGE: JOHN 19:25, ALONG WITH
MATTHEW 27:55–56, MARK 15:40–41, AND
LUKE 23:49

Focus verse: *Near the cross of Jesus stood his mother, his mother's sister, Mary the wife of Clopas, and Mary Magdalene.* (John 19:25)

In our biblical narrative we don't move directly from Jesus's death to his resurrection. There's much that happens between these two events. We'll spend the next six days looking at them. We start with the women at the cross who keep vigil with Jesus as he suffers and dies.

John names four of them: Jesus's mother, Mary; his aunt (Mary's sister); Mary, who's married to Clopas; and Mary Magdalene.

We expect Jesus's mother, Mary, to be there, as any mother would. She couldn't prevent his suffering and can't ease his pain. But she can support him by being present. Sometimes the best way—the only way—to care for someone when they suffer is to be present. Mary does that for her son.

Mary's sister, Jesus's aunt, is there too. This is the only time the Bible mentions her. Is she there for Jesus or for her sister? Either way, we applaud her caring nature.

Next is Mary, the wife of Clopas. The Bible gives us no more information about either of them. We may bristle at Mary's identity being tied to her husband, but it could be more a notation of convenience rather than significance, since there are many women named Mary in the New Testament. Regardless, Clopas does nothing noteworthy in the Bible, but his wife, Mary, does. She valiantly keeps watch as Jesus suffers and dies.

Scripture tells us that Jesus cast seven demons out of Mary Magdalene. Regardless of how we understand this, we know Jesus made her life much better. In response, Mary Magdalene shows her gratitude by following Jesus and helping support him.

Matthew and Luke don't tell us the names of the women standing watch, but Mark names three. He repeats Mary Magdalene. He adds Mary the mother of James and Joseph, along with Salome, though the Bible tells us nothing more about either of them. Specifically, Mark says these three women followed Jesus and tended to his needs.

And they keep watch as Jesus dies.

These women had come with Jesus from Galilee, his hometown, and cared for him. This might have been practical concerns, such as food, or they may have also provided financial support for him and his disciples. Regardless, they played an integral role in his ministry, even though they weren't counted as disciples.

This is a reminder that a ministry needs a leader, followers, and supporters to succeed. Though we rightly think the most about Jesus and secondarily his disciples, these women play a key role. But they stay in the background, mostly unseen and seldom recognized. Yet without them and their support, Jesus's ministry would not have done as much as it did.

Questions: *How do you function best as a leader, as a follower, and as a supporter? What can you do to better help your spiritual leaders?*

Prayer: Jesus, may we follow you throughout our lives. Show us how we can best support your ministry.

DAY 3: SOLDIERS CONFIRM JESUS'S DEATH

TODAY'S PASSAGE: JOHN 19:31–37

Focus verse: *When they came to Jesus and found that he was already dead, they did not break his legs.* (John 19:33)

At this time, all those at Jesus's cross, both those keeping vigil and those who orchestrated his death, know that Jesus is dead. There's no doubt in their minds. Yet the Jewish leaders don't know this. Most of them weren't at Jesus's cross when he died. This might be because they wanted to distance themselves from being present at the gruesome execution they brought about or to position themselves as though they had nothing to do with it.

John notes that it's the day of Preparation, the day before the Sabbath, and a special Sabbath at that. The religious leaders don't want the three bodies left hanging on the cross during the Sabbath. They want the deceased removed before nightfall. This means the men need to die first, so their corpses can be taken down.

This hearkens back to the law of Moses that talks about capital punishment. The criminal's dead body is to be exposed on a pole, but it's not to be left hanging there overnight. Anyone hung on the pole is under God's curse, and to leave them there is a desecration to the land God will give them (Deuteronomy 21:22–23).

Therefore, the Jewish leaders don't want the bodies on the cross during the Sabbath. They ask Pilate to have the legs of the three men broken, so they'll die quickly and can be taken down from their poles.

These soldiers know death. It's their job to execute criminals. Should they not carry out their duty, they could end up suffering through their own execution. They will not assume someone's dead when they're still alive.

The soldiers break the legs of the rebel on

Jesus's right and then his left. And though none of them see the need to break the legs of a man already dead, one soldier—either out of thoroughness or sport—jabs his spear into Jesus's side, bringing forth a surge of blood and water.

John states he witnessed it. He gives testimony that the soldiers confirmed Jesus's death. As a result, we can believe that Jesus did, in fact, die.

John notes that Scripture foretold the details of Jesus's death. One is that none of his bones would be broken (Psalm 34:20).

Another prophecy states that his body has been pierced. The prophet goes on to write that they will mourn his death as one grieves the death of an only child, of a firstborn son (Zechariah 12:10).

This precisely identifies Jesus. In a spiritual sense, he's God's only child. In a physical sense, he's Joseph and Mary's firstborn son. And they grieve over his passing.

Questions: *How do we grieve Jesus's death? Knowing that Jesus will soon rise from the dead, how long should we focus on his passing?*

Prayer: Jesus, may we forever be in awe of what you did when you suffered and died for us on the cross.

DAY 4: JOSEPH OF ARIMATHEA

TODAY'S PASSAGE: JOHN 19:38–42, ALONG
WITH MATTHEW 27:57–61, MARK 15:42–47,
AND LUKE 23:50–56

Focus verse: *Joseph of Arimathea asked Pilate for the
body of Jesus. Now Joseph was a disciple of Jesus, but
secretly because he feared the Jewish leaders.* (John 19:38)

With the confirmation of Jesus's death, we're one step closer to having his body removed from the cross and buried before nightfall. This is so he's not hanging there on the Sabbath. Though obeying this law of Moses concerns the religious leaders, they do little to make it happen, other than to ask Pilate to have Jesus's legs broken to ensure his death.

This is where Joseph from Arimathea comes in. He provides for the burial of Jesus. Scripture only mentions him on this one occasion, albeit in all four of Jesus's biographies.

As a result, we know little about Joseph, but we do know four facts.

First, he's wealthy enough to have his own rock-hewn burial vault.

Next, he is a prominent member of the Jewish Council. He waits in expectation for the kingdom of God. Although all Hebrews look forward to the prophesied Savior, Joseph is more open to see God at work.

Third, Joseph is a disciple of Jesus. But he keeps his faith a secret because he fears what would happen to him should other Council members find out.

Last, Joseph had not agreed with the Council's decision to execute Jesus (Luke 23:51).

Not wanting to see Jesus's body remain on the cross during the Sabbath, Joseph asks Pilate for permission to give Jesus a proper burial. This tells us that Joseph is bold when it counts.

Though he may have used care to hide his personal beliefs from the Council, requesting Jesus's body for burial further aligns Joseph with Jesus. There is now little doubt about Joseph's priorities.

With this public stance, Joseph takes an enormous risk. The Council could expel him, his friends could shun him, and he could suffer like Jesus, even die. We don't know if any of these concerns happen to Joseph, but we also don't read anything more about him in Scripture.

Joseph, along with Nicodemus, removes Jesus's body from the cross. They prepare his corpse for burial, using seventy pounds of spices. The pair wrap his body in strips of linen. Having prepared his body, they place it in Joseph's tomb and roll a large stone in front of the opening. They do this in haste because it's the day of Preparation.

Questions: *What risks are we willing to take to do what's right for Jesus? What lessons can we learn from Joseph of Arimathea?*

Prayer: Lord, may we have the courage to be bold for you.

DAY 5: NICODEMUS
TODAY'S PASSAGE: JOHN 19:39

Focus verse: *[Joseph] was accompanied by Nicodemus, the man who earlier had visited Jesus at night.* (John 19:39)

John writes that a man named Nicodemus helps Joseph of Arimathea bury Jesus's body. In his biography of Jesus, John records three passages about Nicodemus, but he's the only gospel writer to do so.

Like Joseph, Nicodemus is a Pharisee and a member of the Jewish Council.

The first time we hear about Nicodemus is when he meets with Jesus at night, under the anonymity of darkness (John 3:1–21). This reveals he doesn't want other Pharisees or fellow Council members to know he's talking to Jesus, a man most of them hate. Jesus irritates them, threatening their religious practices, their way of life, and their tenuous standing with their Roman overseers.

Yet Nicodemus desperately wants to talk to Jesus. But he's careful, afraid of the repercussions should the religious leaders find out. Because of his fear, he creeps through the darkness of night to meet Jesus.

After Nicodemus commends Jesus, Jesus answers a question his visitor hasn't asked. Jesus says, "You must be born again if you hope to see the kingdom of God."

"What? How can a person be born a second time? That's impossible!"

Jesus tells Nicodemus about the importance of being born of water *and* the Spirit (John 3:5). While flesh gives birth to flesh, the Spirit gives birth to spirit. There are earthly things and heavenly things. Jesus reminds Nicodemus of Moses lifting the bronze snake in the wilderness to save the people (Numbers 21:8–9).

Likewise, the Son of Man (that is, Jesus) must be lifted to save the people too. Everyone who believes will have eternal life. Jesus ends by talking about truth and light. In doing so, he implies Nicodemus should stop sneaking around in the dark (John 3:1–21). John, however, doesn't tell us how Nicodemus reacts to Jesus's teaching.

The second account of Nicodemus occurs after the religious leaders send the temple guards to arrest Jesus. They're unsuccessful. As the religious leaders criticize the guards for their failure, Nicodemus lobbies for a fair hearing for Jesus. But they don't follow Nicodemus's advice. Instead, they verbally attack him (John 7:45–52).

A few days later, we see John's third and final account of Nicodemus in today's passage. This time Nicodemus goes with Joseph to give Jesus's body a proper burial. It's Nicodemus who supplies the seventy pounds of spices, a mixture of myrrh and aloes, to prepare Jesus for burial. They place Jesus's body in Joseph's tomb.

This is a bold risk for Nicodemus, just as it is for Joseph, with Nicodemus facing the same ramifications as his partner. Though the Bible never tells us if Nicodemus is born again, this last story confirms he's moving in that direction.

Questions: *Which of the three stories of Nicodemus do we most identify with? What can we learn from Nicodemus and Joseph working together?*

Prayer: Heavenly Father, show us who we should work with, either because they need our help or because we need theirs.

DAY 6: WATCHING JESUS'S BURIAL
TODAY'S PASSAGE: MATTHEW 27:61, MARK
15:47, AND LUKE 23:55–56

Focus verse: *The women who had come with Jesus from Galilee followed Joseph and saw the tomb and how his body was laid in it.* (Luke 23:55)

Jesus is dead and buried. Joseph of Arimathea and Nicodemus removed his body from the cross, prepared it for burial, and laid it in the tomb. They did this out of reverence for Jesus, but they also had to do it quickly, so they could finish their task before the Sabbath—when they're prohibited from doing any work.

Some of the women who followed Jesus from Galilee watch this happen. Though Luke identifies them generically as "the women," Matthew and Mark tell us it's Mary Magdalene and the "other Mary," who may also be known as Mary, the mother of Joseph. There may have been others watching with them too, but if so, we don't know who. We may, however, speculate they're from the group of six who kept vigil at Jesus's cross as he died (Day 2).

Joseph and Nicodemus prepared Jesus's body for burial using a mixture of myrrh and aloes. Yet the women who see the pair place Jesus in the tomb leave to prepare their own spices and perfumes.

Why do they do this?

It could be they don't realize the extent of Joseph and Nicodemus's work. Or that since they did their work in haste to complete it before the Sabbath, they may have not fully finished all they needed, or wanted, to do. Or it may be the ladies don't think the men did it right.

Regardless, they leave to prepare their own concoction of spices and perfumes for Jesus. Yet the Sabbath also cuts their work short. They rest on the seventh day, as the Old Testament commands (Exodus 31:15 and Leviticus 16:31).

Once the Sabbath is over, they'll return to Jesus's tomb to complete their work.

But as they wait, as they spend their day of rest, what must they be thinking? Jesus, this man they followed and placed their hope in, is dead. And all their expectations for the future died with him.

What will they do next? What will happen to his disciples—his followers—and the core group of ladies who supported him so diligently? Can they return to their life as it once was?

Mary Magdalene certainly doesn't want to do that. Before Jesus, demons controlled her. She's known what life was like with demons, and she's experienced life with Jesus. But she's never known life without demons *and* without Jesus. What will her life look like?

Questions: *When have we felt a need to redo what someone else has already done? When we take a day of rest, do our thoughts draw us to God or cause us to worry about the future?*

Prayer: Lord, when we don't know what to do next, show us the way.

DAY 7: GUARDING THE TOMB

TODAY'S PASSAGE: MATTHEW 27:62–66

Focus verse: *"Take a guard," Pilate answered. "Go, make the tomb as secure as you know how."* (Matthew 27:65)

Once Jesus's body is in the tomb, some of the religious leaders have another concern. They remember Jesus saying that after three days, he would rise from the dead. They share Jesus's words with Pilate.

Though they have no expectation that Jesus might really come back to life, it occurs to them that his disciples may steal his body. With his tomb empty, they could claim he had, in fact, risen from the dead.

This, they reason, would be an even worse deception than him claiming he was the Son of God.

Pilate tells them to take a guard and make the tomb as secure as possible. They do what Pilate said, putting a seal on the stone and posting a watch.

What isn't clear is if they do this with Roman soldiers or with their own temple guards. It would be easiest for them to use their own staff, but why would they come to Pilate? Roman soldiers, with their training and experience, would be more skilled to do this.

Though we don't know who supplies security, we do know they place a seal over the stone that blocks the tomb's entrance. This seal isn't like a chain or a lock to prevent the stone from being moved, but it functions as evidence to show if someone tampers with the stone. They also post a guard. From this text, we don't know whether this is a solitary soldier or a group of them, though we'll later learn there were multiple men guarding Jesus's tomb.

From this account, we have two interesting considerations.

The first is, why do the Jewish leaders who

oppose Jesus clearly remember his statement that he will die and three days later rise again? Jesus's own followers don't comprehend this. Or at least their actions show they don't. It's not until later when they recall what he said.

The other item to ponder is that the religious leaders don't even consider the fact that Jesus might actually rise from the dead. During his ministry, he brought other people back to life: the son of a widow from Nain, Jairus's daughter, and, most notably, Lazarus. The religious leaders know about Jesus resurrecting the four-day-dead Lazarus and how this miracle caused many people to believe in Jesus. The religious leaders are so distraught over this that they want to kill Lazarus too (John 12:10–11, 17).

If Jesus can resurrect Lazarus, couldn't he also resurrect himself? Yet the religious leaders don't accept this as a possibility. And neither do Jesus's followers, at least not yet.

Questions: *Why do those who oppose Jesus remember what he said when his own followers don't? What do we do with the things Jesus says that we don't understand?*

Prayer: Holy Spirit, reveal to us what the words of Jesus mean.

DAY 8: RETURNING TO THE TOMB

TODAY'S PASSAGE: JOHN 20:1, ALONG WITH
MATTHEW 28:1, MARK 16:1–3, AND LUKE 24:1

Focus verse: *Early on the first day of the week, while it*
was still dark, Mary Magdalene went to the tomb. (John
20:1)

With the Sabbath over, Mary Magdalene can again do manual labor. She returns to Jesus's tomb, intending to anoint his body. She and the other Mary prepared spices before the Sabbath, rested on the Sabbath, and now she's ready to complete her work on the first day of the week.

Mark gives us the most detail about what happens.

He writes that besides Mary Magdalene, Mary

the mother of James (possibly also called *the other Mary*) and Salome go with her. It's early in the day, with the sun having just risen. As the trio makes their way to the tomb, a critical concern occurs to them. "Who will roll away the stone from the tomb?"

Who indeed.

Just two days earlier, the women stood there watching Joseph of Arimathea and Nicodemus place Jesus's body in the tomb and roll a large stone in front of the entrance. Did the women forget this important detail until this moment? Or did they realize it and decide to keep their concern to themselves? Perhaps each one hopes one of the other two has a plan to remove this obstacle.

But the three of them are no match for this massive stone. They won't be able to move it by themselves. Unless someone else does this for them, they cannot complete their mission. This would make their preparations and journey in vain.

Despite not knowing what they'll do, however, they press forward. Do they expect to find someone there to help them? Do they pray God will provide a solution to their dilemma? Might they have a backup plan if they can't get to Jesus's body this morning?

Whatever the case, they proceed. What other choice do they have? They can't quit. Jesus deserves better.

Questions: *When have we planned something without considering the obstacles we would face? How do we react when we find a stone blocking our path?*

Prayer: Father God, when we face obstacles on the path you give us, fill us with the needed courage—and the faith—to persist.

DAY 9: THE STONE IS ROLLED AWAY

TODAY'S PASSAGE: JOHN 20:1, ALONG WITH
MATTHEW 28:2–4, MARK 16:4, AND LUKE 24:2–
3

Focus verse: *Mary Magdalene went to the tomb and saw that the stone had been removed from the entrance.* (John 20:1)

John, Mark, and Luke all simply write that when Mary Magdalene and her friends arrive at the tomb, they find the stone has been rolled away. They state this as fact and without explanation. The women's question of "Who will roll away the stone?" becomes a nonissue for them when they arrive. Someone has moved that obstacle from their path.

Yet Matthew gives us the explanation we seek and in the most dramatic fashion. There's an earthquake. This is the second one in a couple of days. Recall our reading in the prologue. When Jesus dies, the earth quakes, graves open, and the bodies of holy people come to life.

Now there's a second quake. Matthew calls it a violent one. God's angel comes down from heaven, goes to the tomb, and rolls away the stone that blocks the entrance. This is easy for him to do. The angel sits on the stone. He glows like lightning and his clothes are white like freshly fallen snow. What an impressive sight.

I imagine him sitting on his perch, sporting a self-satisfied look of accomplishment. I sense a bit of a smirk, assuming angels may do such a thing.

Matthew doesn't tell us how Mary Magdalene and her friends react to the angel and what he did. Yet we can imagine a sense of astonishment and fear, mixed with relief.

We know the women wondered who would roll away the stone so they could access the tomb (Mark 16:3). They may have considered who they could seek for help. Or they may have prayed for God to send someone to assist them. He certainly did, but not how they expected. God didn't send a person to roll away the stone for them—he sent one of his angels.

Though we don't know the women's reaction, Matthew does tell us about the guards. They tremble at the tomb in fear. They become frozen as if they're dead.

The women see that Jesus's body isn't there. It's missing. They don't yet realize he has risen from the dead, just as he promised.

Questions: *How often does God answer our prayers in a way we don't expect? How often do we pray for a supernatural answer instead of a natural one?*

Prayer: Heavenly Father, may we seek you when we have a need and thank you for your provisions in whatever way you provide them.

DAY 10: THE ANGELS' MESSAGE

TODAY'S PASSAGE: MATTHEW 28:5–7, MARK
16:5–7, AND LUKE 24:4–8

Focus verse: *"He is not here; he has risen, just as he
said."* (Matthew 28:6)

In Matthew's account of what happens, the angel—the one sitting on the stone—says to the women, "Don't be afraid." As we read throughout Scripture, this is often the first thing angels say to the people they encounter.

"You're looking for Jesus who was crucified," the angel continues, "but he's not here. He has risen from the dead, just like he told you he would." The angel guides the women into the tomb where Jesus's dead body once lay, but it is no longer there.

Mark's version is a bit different. He writes that

the women enter the open tomb and see the angel *inside*. He says, "Don't be alarmed" and repeats the same message about the body of crucified Jesus no longer being in the tomb because he's risen from the dead.

"Go and tell his disciples—and Peter—that he's going ahead of them into Galilee," the angel says. "They'll find him there, just as he said."

It's comforting to hear the angel single out Peter. To know the angel's message of Jesus's resurrection also includes him must be most reassuring. After denying that he even knew Jesus, Peter must wonder where he stands with his Rabbi. Now he knows—thanks to the angel's message—that Jesus still wants to see him, to be with him.

For his account, Luke mentions two angels. Though we might think of these three accounts as being misaligned, even contradictory, remember where Matthew and Mark place their angels.

In Matthew's version the angel sits outside the tomb on the stone. In Mark's version the angel is inside the tomb. What if they are two different angels, one outside the tomb and the other inside?

For their part, Luke's two angels give the same message as we read in Matthew and Mark's accounts. Their message is what matters most, not if there are one or two of them or where they are.

The angels remind the women that Jesus predicted he would be crucified and three days later rise from the dead. As soon as the women hear this, they remember what he said. But they still have trouble believing it—at least for now.

Questions: *How should we react when Scripture seems to contradict itself, as with Matthew, Mark, and Luke's accounts of the angels at the empty tomb? How content are we to accept that in this world we will never understand everything in the Bible—or about God?*

Prayer: Holy Spirit, speak to us and guide our thoughts as we read, study, and meditate on the Bible.

DAY 11: MARY TELLS PETER AND JOHN

TODAY'S PASSAGE: JOHN 20:2–9, ALONG WITH LUKE 24:12

Focus verse: *"They have taken the Lord out of the tomb, and we don't know where they have put him!"* (John 20:2)

At this point Mary Magdalene knows the tomb is empty, but she doesn't realize Jesus has risen from the dead. Her logical assumption is that someone moved his body.

This makes even more sense when we remember that Joseph of Arimathea and Nicodemus hastily placed Jesus's body in the tomb so they could complete their task before the Sabbath. It's reasonable for her to conclude that they came and moved his body to a more permanent resting place.

Even so, she's upset and wants to share this distressing news with someone. We don't know if she seeks Peter out or if he's merely the first disciple she finds, but he's the one she tells—along with John.

We can envision her running up to them, panting and breathlessly blurting out what she saw —or, more correctly, what she assumes. "Someone moved Jesus's body, and we don't know where they put it!"

Notice she says *we*. Though John only mentions Mary, other biographies of Jesus tell us several women saw the open and empty tomb. We don't know if they trailed behind Mary to share this news or if only Mary is brave enough to do so.

Peter and John sprint to the tomb. John outruns Peter and arrives first. He peers inside the empty crypt and sees only the linen burial cloths, but he doesn't enter. We don't know if he hesitates out of respect for Jesus's gravesite or out of a reluctance to be in an area reserved for death.

However, when impetuous Peter arrives, he brushes past John and charges in. He sees the burial linens as well, along with a separate cloth that was wrapped around Jesus's head.

At last John goes inside the burial vault too. He sees the empty tomb and believes.

But what does he believe?

He still doesn't understand that Jesus has risen from the dead. What he believes is Mary's report that Jesus's body is no longer there.

Questions: *With spiritual matters, are we more like cautious John or impetuous Peter? Why do you think it's so hard for Mary, Peter, and John to realize Jesus has risen from the dead, just as he told them would happen?*

Prayer: Heavenly Father, when we read your Word, may we have the faith to believe what it says —even if it doesn't align with our assumptions.

DAY 12: BRIBING THE GUARDS
TODAY'S PASSAGE: MATTHEW 28:11–15

Focus verse: *Some of the guards went into the city and reported to the chief priests everything that had happened.* (Matthew 28:11)

As Mary runs to tell Jesus's disciples that she doesn't know where his body is, some of the guards assigned to stand watch over the tomb go to the chief priests to report everything that had happened.

What, exactly, do they tell the religious leaders?

Though they could simply say that Jesus's body is missing, this would provoke more questions and make the guards look negligent. Surely, they tell the complete story. Looking at Matthew's account, we know of an earthquake and an angel coming to roll away the stone—and breaking the seal. Once his task is complete, he sits on the stone, blazing like lightning. The guards freeze in fear, like dead men (Matthew 28:2–4).

This is what *some* of the guards report. What about the rest? Are they still frozen in fear? Have they run away, trying to get as far as they can from these terrifying events? We don't know.

What we do know is that *some* guards report to the religious leaders. They may be conscientious, or they may be trying their best to protect themselves from charges of misconduct and the punishment they could receive.

Though what they say sounds incredible, the chief priests believe them. The religious leaders meet to decide what to do. Regardless of what happened, an empty tomb is exactly what they don't want to deal with.

They can't deny it's empty, so they concoct a false narrative and attempt to rewrite history. They bribe the guards—with a "large sum of money"—to lie, to say they fell asleep, and Jesus's disciples stole his body. The religious leaders also pledge to cover for the guards if this report gets back to Pilate, the governor.

This points to the corruption of the religious leaders. They don't care about the truth. They don't care to do what is right. This shouldn't surprise us. They already paid Judas thirty pieces of silver to betray Jesus. And when he tried to return it, they wouldn't take it back because they called it blood money (Matthew 27:3–6).

As for the soldiers, they take the simple way out and accept the bribe. They lie. The report circulates widely, and the Jewish people believe it.

Questions: *When have we perpetuated a lie? Are we more interested in doing what is right or what is easy?*

Prayer: Lord, may we have the integrity to do what is right regardless of the consequences.

DAY 13: JESUS APPEARS TO MARY MAGDALENE

TODAY'S PASSAGE: JOHN 20:10–16, ALONG
WITH MATTHEW 28:9 AND MARK 16:9

Focus verse: *Jesus said to her, "Mary."* (John 20:16)

After Peter and John see the empty tomb, they leave and return to where they're staying. Mary doesn't. She lingers. She needs closure, and leaving won't provide that. Tears of remorse and confusion overwhelm her. Crying is the only thing she can do.

Jesus is dead (or so she thinks), Peter and John have left her, and she is alone. Mary doesn't know what her future will be like. It may be the darkest moment of her life, even worse than when she had seven demons tormenting her—the affliction Jesus had driven from her, freeing her from their control. But now what?

She looks inside the tomb again and sees two angels. They sit where Jesus's body had lain, one at his head and the other at the foot. "Why are you crying?" they ask.

Mary again shares her assumption of what happened. "They've taken my Lord's body, and I don't know where they put it."

At this point, something causes her to turn around.

It's Jesus, but she doesn't recognize him. "Why are you crying?" he also asks. "Who are you looking for?" These are Jesus's first recorded words since he rose from the dead.

Mary assumes he's the gardener. She repeats her plea that he'll tell her where he put Jesus's body.

Jesus doesn't directly respond. This isn't because he's dismissing her angst, but because she's seeking the wrong thing. Instead, his one-word reply tells her everything she needs to know.

He says her name. I'm sure it comes out in a most gentle and soothing way. "Mary."

At that moment, everything changes for her. Relief overwhelms her. He's alive. He has risen from the grave. She cries out "Rabboni!", which means "Teacher."

Mary Magdalene is the first person our risen Savior reveals himself to. It's not to the eleven remaining disciples. It's not to his mother. It's not to John, the disciple he loves, and it's not to Peter, who desperately needs Jesus's reassurance that his denial of his master is forgiven.

It is to Mary.

Jesus chooses Mary to be the first person to see him in resurrected form. In doing so, he honors Mary. And he elevates her witness, something that society would dismiss.

As we delight in the truth that Jesus first shows himself to Mary Magdalene—before all others—let us not forget the first things our resurrected Savior says. Though he says them to Mary, his words are also for us: "Why are you crying?" and "Who are you looking for?"

When we cry, Jesus is there to comfort us. When we search, Jesus is waiting.

Questions: *When have we cried out? What (or who) are we searching for?*

Prayer: Jesus, thank you for hearing us when we cry.

DAY 14: MARY MAGDALENE TELLS THE DISCIPLES

TODAY'S PASSAGE: JOHN 20:17–18, ALONG WITH MATTHEW 28:10, MARK 16:10–11, AND LUKE 24:9–11

Focus verse: *Mary Magdalene went to the disciples with the news: "I have seen the Lord!"* (John 20:18)

Mary has seen the resurrected Jesus. He talked to her and she, with him. In relief, she moves toward him, but he says, "Don't touch me, for I have not yet ascended to my Father."

If we struggle to understand what Jesus means, we're not alone. As we'll soon learn, he'll later encourage Thomas to touch him, to feel his scars. So why does he tell Mary not to touch him?

One interpretation is that Jesus does so to mark a delineation between his physical self, which Mary knew prior to his death, and his spiritual self, which he'll fully reclaim once he ascends to heaven. He is not a physical Messiah but a supernatural one.

Jesus sends Mary on an important mission to tell his brothers—his disciples and followers—about his resurrection. He tasks a woman, whose testimony that day's society won't accept, to deliver the most important news throughout history, that Jesus is alive!

The Gospel of John records one part of this message, that Jesus will soon ascend to his Father and their Father, to his God and their God. (Yet this won't happen for a few weeks.)

Matthew records another aspect of the message Jesus wants Mary to give to his followers. After assuring her to not be afraid, he says, "Tell my brothers to go to Galilee, and there they'll see me."

Did you catch that?

Jesus wants to meet his disciples in Galilee. Galilee isn't close to Jerusalem. Jesus is from the area of Galilee and so are most of his disciples. Jesus's first recorded miracle is at a wedding in Cana, which is in Galilee (John 2:1–11). Galilee serves as Jesus's home base during his three-year ministry. It's also where the Sea of Galilee is.

Since Galilee is a region and not a precise location, we can only approximate the distance from Jerusalem to Galilee, but it's about seventy miles (113 kilometers). It would take three to four days to walk that far. Yet that's where Jesus wants his disciples to go. Not only does he tell this to Mary now, but he even told it to his disciples before he died (Mark 14:28).

However, when Mary (and the other women with her) delivers Jesus's message to the disciples, they don't believe her. It makes little sense to them, despite Jesus's prior assurances that he would rise from the dead after his crucifixion and even though Peter and John can confirm Jesus's tomb is empty.

Questions: *How do we react when people don't believe us? How do we respond when someone tells us about something supernatural that doesn't make sense?*

Prayer: Jesus, may we hear what you say and do what you tell us.

DAY 15: TWO TO EMMAUS

TODAY'S PASSAGE: MARK 16:12–13 AND LUKE
24:13–18

Focus verse: *As they talked and discussed these things
with each other, Jesus himself came up and walked along
with them.* (Luke 24:15)

John doesn't mention that two of Jesus's followers make a trip to Emmaus. While Mark mentions this briefly, Luke gives us the full story. And a most delightful story it is. It's so packed with interesting details that we'll take the next several days to cover it.

Luke tells us that the same day of Jesus's resurrection, two of his followers head for the town of Emmaus. This is the only passage in the Bible to mention Emmaus. All we know about it is that it's seven miles (10 kilometers) from Jerusalem. It would take about three hours to walk.

One of the two men is Cleopas. The Bible doesn't tell us any more about him either. But at least we know his name, which is more than we can say for his traveling companion.

As they walk along, they talk about what's on their mind. Jesus, the man they followed as the expected Messiah, died. This single predominant thought preoccupies them.

Like Mary Magdalene, they wonder what to do next. This may even be why they're headed to Emmaus. It might be where they're from. At the very least, they have friends or family there. How dejected they must feel as they plod along on their journey.

And as they walk, Jesus comes up alongside them and joins them on their trip. But they don't recognize him. It may be they don't see him because they don't expect to. In their mind he is dead. Or perhaps his appearance in resurrected form is different enough to confuse them. Or maybe Jesus blocks them from seeing who he really is.

Regardless, he asks what they're discussing.

They stop walking, their faces downcast.

Incredulous, Cleopas asks the man if he's the only one visiting Jerusalem who doesn't know what happened.

By design, a Roman crucifixion was a public event. They wanted everyone to know what happens to dissidents and troublemakers. This knowledge would serve as a most effective deterrent for anyone who wanted to oppose Roman rule.

In addition, Jesus was a public figure. Surely everyone in the area knew of his crucifixion—everyone, that is, except for this mysterious stranger.

Questions: *How do we respond to someone we meet who doesn't know about Jesus? How do we react when our life takes an unexpected turn, as it did for Cleopas and his friend?*

Prayer: Jesus, when we don't know what to do, may we always turn to you.

DAY 16: THE PAIR TELL JESUS WHAT HE DID

TODAY'S PASSAGE: LUKE 24:19–24

Focus verse: *"He was a prophet, powerful in word and deed before God and all the people."* (Luke 24:19)

Jesus pretends he doesn't know what the men are talking about. Though I'm uncomfortable saying that Jesus plays dumb, that's essentially what he does. "What things?" he asks.

The pair give the man—whom they don't yet recognize as Jesus—a concise summary of what happened. They tell Jesus who he was and what he did.

We're talking about Jesus of Nazareth (which is part of Galilee). "He was a prophet," they say. "He was powerful in word and in deed." In this way, they affirm the words he said and the things he did, such as healing people, casting out demons, and performing miracles. This includes turning water into wine and multiplying food.

"He did this before both God and the people," they say. Though they don't know the mind of God, they perceive Jesus's actions pleased the Almighty, just as he received the acclaim of those who heard him speak and saw his supernatural acts.

Despite all this, they say, "Our religious leaders had him crucified." Let this sink in. Jesus is a Jew. He comes to his own people—other Jews—to save them, just as their prophets had proclaimed. But the Jewish religious leaders don't see this and kill him. To them they are merely solving a problem.

Then the men give their testimony. "We hoped he was the prophesied one who would redeem Israel, to deliver our nation from oppression." They get this part mostly right, but, like everyone else, they think Jesus will redeem them physically instead of spiritually.

The pair's outlook may brighten a bit. "His crucifixion happened three days ago, but some women in our group shocked us this morning. They went to his tomb. It was empty! But there were angels who said he is alive and no longer dead. Two guys in our group confirmed what the ladies said. The tomb was empty, and Jesus's body isn't there."

After saying this, an inexplicable hope must rise in them, wondering what it all means.

Questions: *How ready are we to tell others about Jesus? Where do we really place our hope?*

Prayer: Lord Jesus, may the hope we place in you remain steady and never waver.

DAY 17: OLD TESTAMENT PROPHECY
TODAY'S PASSAGE: LUKE 24:25–27

Focus verse: *Beginning with Moses and all the Prophets, [Jesus] explained to them what was said in all the Scriptures concerning himself.* (Luke 24:27)

After hearing the two men tell Jesus about himself, the Savior responds. He begins with some harsh criticism. He calls them foolish and slow to believe. They should have known the Messiah would suffer as he did and rise to glory.

Though Jesus rebukes these two men, it equally applies to the disciples and the women at the tomb. Without exception, each one of them is slow to believe what the prophets wrote.

Jesus reviews what Moses and the prophets said about him, but Luke doesn't give any details. I wish he had. There are too many prophecies to consider. Bible scholars list over three hundred Old Testament prophecies about Jesus.

Here are some of the top ones. Jesus will:

- Be born of a virgin, from Isaiah 7:14, which is fulfilled in Matthew 1:22–23.
- Be born in Bethlehem, from Micah 5:2, which is fulfilled in Luke 2:4–6.
- Come from the tribe of Judah, from Genesis 49:10, which is verified in Matthew 1:3–16.
- Come out of Egypt, from Hosea 11:1, which is confirmed in Matthew 2:14–15.
- Be heir of King David and rule on his throne forever, from 2 Samuel 7:12–13 and Isaiah 9:7, which is validated in Luke 1:32–33.
- Minister in Galilee, from Isaiah 9:1–2, which we find in Matthew 4:13–16.
- Proclaim good news, from Isaiah 61:1–2, which is fulfilled in Luke 4:18–19.
- Speak in parables, from Psalm 78:2–4,

which is confirmed in Matthew 13:10–15.

- Be a priest forever in the order of Melchizedek, from Psalm 110:4, which is verified in Hebrews 5:5–6.
- Have little children praise him, from Psalm 8:2, which happens in Matthew 21:16.
- Come to them riding a colt, from Zechariah 9:9, which we see in Mark 11:7–11.
- Be betrayed, from Psalm 41:9, which occurs in Luke 22:47–48.
- Be sold for thirty pieces of silver, from Zechariah 11:12–13, which is confirmed in Matthew 26:14–16 and Matthew 27:7–10.
- Be rejected by his own people, from Isaiah 53:3, which is verified in John 1:11 and John 7:5.
- Be falsely accused, from Psalm 35:11, which is confirmed in Mark 14:57–59.
- Be silent before his accusers, from Isaiah 53:7, which is fulfilled in Mark 15:4–5.
- Be spat upon and struck, from Isaiah 50:6, which happens in Matthew 26:67.

- Be hated without cause, from Psalm 35:19 and 69:4, which is verified in John 15:24–25.
- Be crucified with criminals, from Isaiah 53:12, which we see in Matthew 27:38 and Mark 15:27–28.
- Be given vinegar to drink, from Psalm 69:21, which is fulfilled in Matthew 27:34 and John 19:28–30.
- Have his hands and feet pierced, from Psalm 22:16 and Zechariah 12:10, which is confirmed in John 20:25–27.
- Be mocked and ridiculed, from Psalm 22:7–8, which is seen in Luke 23:35.
- Have soldiers gamble for his clothes, from Psalm 22:18, which is verified in Luke 23:34 and Matthew 27:35.
- Be forsaken by God, from Psalm 22:1, which is confirmed in Matthew 27:46.
- Pray for his enemies, from Psalm 109:4, which is seen in Luke 23:34.
- Be a sin sacrifice, from Isaiah 53:5–12, which is confirmed in Romans 5:6–8.
- Have soldiers pierce his side, from Zechariah 12:10, which is fulfilled in John 19:34.

- Not have any bones broken, from Exodus 12:46 and Psalm 34:20, which is fulfilled in John 19:33–36.
- Be buried with the rich, from Isaiah 53:9, which we see in Matthew 27:57–60.
- Will rise from the dead, from Psalm 16:10 and Psalm 49:15, which is verified in Matthew 28:2–7 and Acts 2:22–32.
- Will ascend to heaven, from Psalm 68:18, which happens in Mark 16:19 and Luke 24:51.
- Will sit at God's right hand, from Psalm 110:1, which we read in Mark 16:19 and Matthew 22:44.

In addition to foretelling of Jesus's virgin birth, Isaiah also writes what Jesus will accomplish (Isaiah 9:7), his rule (Isaiah 40:10), him tending to us as a shepherd cares for his sheep (Isaiah 40:11), and his suffering and sacrifice (Isaiah 53).

Ezekiel writes that Jesus, a descendant of David, will be a shepherd (Ezekiel 34:23). Daniel writes about Jesus atoning for sin (Daniel 9:24). Micah says Jesus will descend from Jacob, as God promised (Micah 7:20). And Malachi prophesies that a messenger (John the baptizer) will precede Jesus, come to his temple, and bring a new covenant (Malachi 3:1).

Another reference reminds us of Moses lifting a bronze snake on a pole. Anyone afflicted with a venomous snake bite could look at the figure and be saved (Numbers 21:9). Many see this as an allusion to Jesus's crucifixion on the cross (that is, on a pole) to save all who will look to him. And Moses foresaw God raising up a prophet for the people (Deuteronomy 18:15).

These are just some of the many Old Testament prophecies about Jesus.

Questions: *Which prophecy is most significant to you? What other prophecies would you add to the list?*

Prayer: Father God, thank you for Old Testament prophecy that foretells about Jesus and confirms this was your plan all along.

DAY 18: HOSPITALITY TO STRANGERS

TODAY'S PASSAGE: LUKE 24:28–29

Focus verse: *"Stay with us, for it is nearly evening; the day is almost over." So [Jesus] went in to stay with them.*
(Luke 24:29)

As the trio of men—Cleopas, his friend, and Jesus, the stranger who joined them—continue their journey, they arrive at the village of Emmaus. Cleopas and his friend have reached their destination, but Jesus intends to continue walking.

They urge him to stay with them. "It's almost evening, and the sun is about to set." Jesus agrees, yet the pair still do not recognize him.

We see this idea of hospitality to strangers

modeled in the Old Testament and commanded in the Torah, the law of Moses. Though there's no specific Old Testament instruction to invite travelers into our home for a meal and offer them shelter for the night, the principle is there.

We also see hospitality encouraged in the New Testament. Paul tells the church in Rome to practice hospitality (Romans 12:13). Peter writes that we should offer hospitality to others without grumbling (1 Peter 4:9). And John says that we ought to show hospitality (3 John 1:8).

Paul also celebrates Gaius because he and the whole church have enjoyed his hospitality (Romans 16:23). In his letter to Timothy, Paul identifies hospitality as an example of doing good deeds (1 Timothy 5:10).

The most significant teaching about hospitality, however, comes in the letter to the Hebrews. They're instructed to not forget to show hospitality to strangers. In doing so, some people have unknowingly entertained angels (Hebrews 13:2).

We see this idea of entertaining angels happen to Abraham and Sarah (Genesis 18:1–3), Lot (Genesis 19:1–2), Gideon (Judges 6:11–24), and Manoah (Judges 13:6–21).

Though the two men traveling to Emmaus don't

realize it, the man they offer hospitality to is someone even more important than an angel. It's Jesus, the Son of God.

Though we could end up showing hospitality to angels, unaware of who they are, it's doubtful we would ever do so to Jesus. Or could we? In his parable of the sheep and goats, Jesus says, "Whatever you do for the least of these, you do for me" (Matthew 25:40).

May we serve others as though serving Jesus.

Questions: *How can we show hospitality to strangers? What could happen when we show kindness to those we don't know?*

Prayer: Jesus, may we be mindful to show hospitality to strangers, as if doing so for you.

DAY 19: BREAKING BREAD
TODAY'S PASSAGE: LUKE 24:30–31

Focus verse: *[Jesus] took bread, gave thanks, broke it and began to give it to them.* (Luke 24:30)

The pair of men traveling to Emmaus invite Jesus to stay with them, but they still haven't recognized him. We don't know if the men are at one of their own houses or if they show up at the home of a family member or friend. In any event, they're hungry after their journey and sit down to eat.

It's interesting that Jesus, as a guest in this home, takes charge to begin the meal. Though they may have offered him this as a courtesy to their guest, it strikes me as presumptuous.

Regardless, Jesus does three things. First, he gives thanks to the Almighty for the bread. Next, he divides it into portions. That is, he breaks bread. Third, he gives it to those waiting to eat.

As he does this, their minds may connect this action with what Jesus did a few days earlier when he instituted the practice of Holy Communion by breaking bread and distributing it to them.

Though we commonly think of Jesus eating the Passover meal with his twelve disciples, likely other followers were there too. This may have included Cleopas and his friend.

In Bible times, the most practical way to divide bread for people at a meal was to break it (not slice it). We remember that at the first Lord's Supper Jesus said the bread represented his body, which would soon be broken when he was crucified.

Therefore, at every meal afterward, Jesus's followers would see bread being broken, and it would automatically remind them of his body being broken for them in the ultimate sacrifice.

And if they weren't present at that Passover meal with Jesus, they may have been there when he performed a miracle to feed over five thousand people (Luke 9:16) and later over four thousand more (Mark 8:6). In both cases he did the same thing as he does this night.

Jesus gives thanks, breaks bread, and gives it to them. They recognize him, and he disappears.

Vanishing is not something Jesus could have done in human form, but he's already moving beyond his human existence to reclaim his super-human reality. This means he's no longer limited by a physical body.

Questions: *What does it mean to us when we celebrate the Lord's Supper at church? How often does eating an ordinary meal remind us of Jesus, like it did for Cleopas and his friend?*

Prayer: Holy Spirit, remind us of what Jesus did for us each time we celebrate Holy Communion, as well as each time we eat a meal.

DAY 20: HEARTS BURNING

TODAY'S PASSAGE: LUKE 24:32–35

Focus verse: *"Were not our hearts burning within us while [Jesus] talked with us on the road and opened the Scriptures to us?" (Luke 24:32)*

When Jesus breaks bread, Cleopas and his friend at last recognize him for who he is. Then he disappears.

The pair look at each other, no doubt with a mixture of shock and awe. "Were not our hearts burning within us as he explained Scripture to us on the road?"

Their hearts burned within them. I readily understand what this means but struggle to explain it. Though this is the only verse in the Bible that mentions "hearts burning within us," an Old Testament passage offers a parallel thought.

In one of David's psalms, the King writes, "My heart grew hot within me. While I meditated, the fire burned" (Psalm 39:3). It sounds like King David experienced the same thing as Jesus's two followers.

How might we experience our hearts burning within us today?

One way, as Jesus models in today's passage, is hearing the Word of God. When it's presented well and we're open to receive it, our hearts can burn over the delightful truth contained in Scripture. The Holy Spirit can help us understand a passage in a fresh way, even if we've heard it many times before. This can ignite a fire within us.

We get a second consideration in the preceding verse from King David. When we meditate on God, we can connect with him in the supernatural. We transcend our physical reality and commune with him in the spiritual realm. As we do, our hearts burn with passion for him, overcome with the wonder of who he is. It's a spiritual ecstasy like no other.

A third time when our hearts can burn within us is when we have a meaningful spiritual conversation with other like-minded followers of Jesus.

When two or more of us gather in his name, he is there. He promised us he would be (Matthew 18:20).

This is another time when our hearts can burn within us. Yet for this to occur, we must be intentional. We need to move beyond superficial conversation and be ready to ask probing spiritual questions, as well as being willing to answer them for others.

If these ideas are new to you or beyond what you've ever experienced, do not despair. Ask the Holy Spirit to direct you so you can also have your heart burn within you.

Trust him to do so and wait with expectation for it to occur.

Questions: *Does being with God cause our hearts to burn? When have we been around someone who made our heart burn within us? When might we have been the person who caused other people to have their hearts burn within them?*

Prayer: Lord, may our hearts burn when we consider who you are and what you've done for us.

DAY 21: TELLING OTHERS
TODAY'S PASSAGE: LUKE 24:33–35

Focus verse: *The two told what had happened on the way, and how Jesus was recognized by them when he broke the bread.* (Luke 24:35)

After Cleopas and his friend see Jesus disappear before their eyes, they talk about how their hearts burned as he taught them through Scripture. Right away they decide to return to Jerusalem. They're excited to tell the disciples what happened.

Remember, it's already late in the day. They had urged Jesus to stay with them and not travel any further. He agreed.

By now, it's even later. It's past time when they

should be on the road. With certain darkness having fallen, the trek back to Jerusalem would not be easy. They would need to navigate an uneven road with little or no light. And it would take another three hours, or longer, because of the nighttime conditions.

The smart thing would be to wait until morning. Yet they can't. They're eager to tell the other disciples they've seen Jesus. Disregarding what is prudent—and their own safety—they trek back.

They find the disciples, but before they can share their news, the disciples have news of their own. "It's true!" they say. "The Lord has risen and appeared to Simon Peter."

If you don't remember Jesus appearing separately to Peter, I don't either. The Bible doesn't record that meeting for us. But Luke writes that it happened and that the disciples know about it. Also, we're left wondering when it occurred. We only know it happened before the pair returned from Emmaus.

Maybe when Jesus disappeared from Cleopas and his friend, he immediately reappeared before Peter. Or it could be the other way around, with Jesus reconnecting with his wayward disciple and then joining the pair traveling to Emmaus.

Based on this, however, we know Jesus has now appeared to four people. First to Mary Magdalene. Next to Peter, and then to Cleopas and his friend. He's yet to reveal his risen self to the other disciples, but at least they accept that he has risen. It's sad that they didn't accept Mary Magdalene's word on this alone, but when Peter confirms Jesus is alive, it's enough for them to believe.

And now Cleopas and his friend verify what Mary and Peter said. This gives us the testimony of four people, three of which the culture of that day legally accepts.

By revealing himself first to Mary Magdalene and sending her to tell the other disciples, it seems Jesus wants to change society's practice of only accepting the testimony of men. Though this is an important lesson here, it's also ancillary.

The main point is that Jesus's followers are at last beginning to accept that he has risen from the dead. Though it may have taken them a while to believe, at last they do.

Believing in Jesus is what matters, regardless of how long it takes.

Questions: *What can we do to help others believe in Jesus? When others dismiss what we say—like what happened to Mary—what should we do?*

Prayer: Jesus, give us courage to tell others about you so that they may believe.

DAY 22: JESUS APPEARS TO THE DISCIPLES

TODAY'S PASSAGE: JOHN 20:19–20, ALONG WITH MARK 16:14 AND LUKE 24:36–43

Focus verse: *Jesus came and stood among them and said, "Peace be with you!"* (John 20:19)

Having spent several days focusing on Luke's account of the pair of disciples who travel to Emmaus, we segue from Luke's gospel back to John's.

Our next story—told by both Luke and John—occurs immediately after Cleopas and his friend tell the disciples about recognizing Jesus when he broke bread for them.

These disciples gather, hiding behind locked doors. They fear the religious leaders. This makes sense. If they killed Jesus, what might they do to his followers who now say he's risen from the dead?

With the doors shut and locked, Jesus materializes before them. This is the opposite of him disappearing in front of Cleopas and his friend. Though Jesus is still in a physical form, there's a supernatural element to his resurrected body.

John writes that Jesus says, "Peace be with you," likely because his sudden appearance terrifies them. He shows them his hands and side, where the wounds from his crucifixion remain. They're overjoyed to see him. Now we can add the rest of the disciples (except for Thomas who we'll later learn isn't there) to the list of people who have seen the risen Savior.

Luke adds additional information to John's account. He writes that Jesus's sudden appearance startles them. They think they've seen a ghost. He gently chastises them. "Why are you so troubled? Why do you allow doubts to creep into your mind?" Then he adds, "Look at my hands and feet. Touch me and see. I am not a ghost." He shows them the wounds on his hands and feet.

Even after this, Luke writes that they still have trouble believing. He eats some food in their presence, as if to confirm he isn't a ghost and really is the risen Jesus.

The addendum to Mark's account is different. It says Jesus rebukes his disciples for their lack of faith and stubborn refusal to believe those who had seen him. Given the context of Mark's narrative, he may refer specifically to them not believing Mary Magdalene's testimony.

Questions: *When have we struggled with a lack of faith? When have we been stubborn to believe what others tell us about Jesus?*

Prayer: Heavenly Father, fill us with faith to fully believe in Jesus and strengthen us to stay true to him through the rest of our lives, regardless of what happens.

DAY 23: UNDERSTANDING SCRIPTURE

TODAY'S PASSAGE: LUKE 24:44–47

Focus verse: *Then he opened their minds so they could understand the Scriptures.* (Luke 24:45)

After Jesus appears to the disciples, Luke records additional details not found in John's account. The risen Savior begins with a polite I-told-you-so reminder to his disciples of what he's already taught them. Succinctly, he says that everything written about him in the Old Testament—that is, the law of Moses, the prophets, and psalms—must be fulfilled.

This reminds us of what Luke wrote about Jesus when he met the pair on the road to Emmaus. There Jesus taught them about himself, starting with Moses and going through all the prophets (Luke 24:27). This time Luke lists a third source, the Psalms. Though Luke doesn't specify which Old Testament passages Jesus quoted, we speculated on some possibilities in Day 17.

Jesus opens their minds so they can understand. It shouldn't surprise us that they need their minds opened, despite having spent three years following Jesus as their Rabbi. The Old Testament confirms this in Isaiah 44:18, and as the prophet foretold (Isaiah 6:10 and Isaiah 32:3).

They have eyes that can't see and ears that can't hear (Jeremiah 5:21 and Ezekiel 12:2).

But now Jesus gives them understanding, so that what was once hidden from them is now seen and heard. I'm sure that, like Cleopas and his friend, the disciples' hearts also burn within them as the Teacher instructs them from Scripture.

Jesus wraps up his teaching with a powerful finale: "Just as the Scriptures say, the Messiah will suffer—that is, he will die—and rise from the grave three days later. The good news of repentance from sins will be proclaimed everywhere, starting in Jerusalem."

The number of people who have seen the risen Savior continues to grow. We're up to thirteen:

Mary Magdalene, Peter, Cleopas and his friend, and nine more disciples. Though we started with twelve disciples, Judas is dead, Simon Peter already knows, and, as we'll later learn, Thomas isn't there.

Questions: *What should we do to make the most out of studying the Bible? Should we ask the Holy Spirit to open our minds to better understand what we read?*

Prayer: Heavenly Father, may we have eyes that see you at work and ears that hear what you want to teach us.

DAY 24: SENDING YOU
TODAY'S PASSAGE: JOHN 20:21–23

Focus verse: *"As the Father has sent me, I am sending you."* (John 20:21)

Jesus again says, "Peace be with you!" He's already said this twice (Luke 24:36 and John 20:19). And he'll say it a fourth time to Thomas in one week (John 20:26). Jesus says this each time he encounters one of his followers in his resurrected form.

He must sense how jarring his unexpected appearance in his risen-from-the-dead body is to his followers, despite having told them he would do exactly that: die and rise from the dead. He wants them to feel peace instead of angst. Filling them with peace to replace their fear will also allow them to better hear what he has to say.

He follows his proclamation of peace by giving them a trio of instructions.

First, he sends them into the world, just as his Father sent him. In short, he commissions them for ministry. John doesn't give us any more information about this, but Matthew, Mark, and Luke all do. We'll cover what they have to say in the days ahead. The point is that Jesus expects them to share the good news of salvation through him with others.

Next, Jesus breathes on his disciples and says, "Receive the Holy Spirit." Just as God breathed physical life into Adam at creation (Genesis 2:7), Jesus now breathes spiritual life into his followers.

Though we might assume the disciples receive this supernatural impartation right away, John doesn't say that. And later we'll see from Luke's writings that it will be a few more weeks before the Holy Spirit arrives and empowers them.

It could be John is taking poetic license and implicitly combining these events here in one passage. Or maybe Jesus is preparing them to receive the Holy Spirit.

But let's not concern ourselves with when or

how they receive it. The essential issue is that they do, in fact, receive the Holy Spirit.

The third thing Jesus says to them seems disconnected from the first two. But it's not. He tells them that if they forgive anyone's sins, those people's sins are forgiven. Conversely, if they do not forgive anyone's sins, those people's sins aren't forgiven.

We shouldn't, however, think that Jesus authorizes them to forgive sins. Only he can do that. Instead, as aligned with the context of this passage, Jesus wants them to tell others about him for the forgiveness of sins.

Those who believe in him will receive forgiveness for their sins. Those who do not believe will not receive his forgiveness.

Questions: *Do we have Jesus's peace within us? Have we received the Holy Spirit? Are we telling others the good news about Jesus?*

Prayer: Jesus, fill us with your peace, the Holy Spirit, and the confidence to tell others about you.

DAY 25: THOMAS SEES JESUS
TODAY'S PASSAGE: JOHN 20:24–29

Focus verse: *Jesus told him, "Because you have seen me, you have believed; blessed are those who have not seen and yet have believed." (John 20:29)*

John now reveals to us that Thomas wasn't present when Jesus first showed himself in resurrected form to the other disciples. Though Matthew, Mark, and Luke tell us little about this disciple, John shares three stories about Thomas.

In the first account (John 14:1–7), Jesus tells his disciples what to expect as his time here on earth winds down, hours prior to his execution. He encourages them to believe in God and in him. He adds that his Father's house has many rooms. "I'll go and prepare them for you. When everything is ready, I'll come back to get you." Then Jesus adds, "You know the way there."

This confuses Thomas. "We don't know where you're going, so how can we know how to get there?"

Jesus responds with a familiar passage. "I am the way, the truth, and the life. To get to Papa, you must go through me." I'm not sure if this explanation satisfies Thomas or if he's afraid to ask any more questions.

We find the next two scenes from Thomas's life covered in today's passage, yet there are two parts to it, occurring at separate times.

The second part is what Thomas is best known for: his lack of faith, as in Doubting Thomas. He isn't present when the risen Savior first appears to his disciples (Day 22). When the other disciples insist Jesus is alive, Thomas is understandably skeptical. He doesn't believe them. He wants proof.

Fortunately, this isn't the end of the story. The next part happens on the first day of the following week. With the disciples again hiding behind locked doors, Jesus supernaturally appears in the room. He approaches Thomas and says, "Peace be with you!"

This is the fourth time he says this to his followers (Day 24).

Jesus shows his doubting disciple the nail scars in his hands. He encourages Thomas to touch his side where the soldier's spear impaled him. "Stop doubting," Jesus says, "and believe."

Thomas does. "My Lord and my God!"

Doubting Thomas becomes Believing Thomas.

Jesus blesses Thomas because he sees and believes. But we're even more blessed because we haven't seen and believe anyway.

Questions: *When it comes to matters of faith, are we more like a doubting Thomas or a believing Thomas? Is faith the absence of doubt or confidence in the face of doubt?*

Prayer: Lord, may we develop a strong faith in you, and may it remain firm throughout our lives.

DAY 26: ANOTHER MIRACULOUS CATCH

TODAY'S PASSAGE: JOHN 21:1–6

Focus verse: *[Jesus] said, "Throw your net on the right side of the boat and you will find some." When they did, they were unable to haul the net in because of the large number of fish.* (John 21:6)

In John's gospel of Jesus, he doesn't mention the disciples traveling to Galilee to meet the resurrected Jesus, but we find them there at the beginning of John 21.

Though Jesus has revealed himself to his disciples, he's not spending all his time with them. In fact, it seems he spends little time with them. This may be to prepare them to continue without him, because he'll soon ascend into heaven and return to reign with his Father.

As such, the disciples may not know what to do. It's not surprising if they're bored and looking for something to fill their time. Seven of them are together: Simon Peter, Thomas, Nathaniel, James and John (the sons of Zebedee), and two others.

Peter tires of sitting around and announces that he's going fishing. In doing so, he reverts to what he knows best, to what he did before Jesus called him to be his follower. The other six men go with him.

They fish all night but catch nothing. Though they had an activity to fill their time, they have nothing to show for their toil. But Jesus uses this situation to get their attention.

Standing on the shore, he calls out and asks if they've caught any fish. They don't recognize him. It's the same as with the pair on the road to Emmaus (Day 15). Even though the disciples have seen Jesus's risen body in the past few days, they don't realize it's him.

"Throw your net on the right side of the boat," Jesus says, "and you'll catch some fish." They do, and suddenly struggle to handle all the fish in their nets.

Does this story sound familiar? The title of

today's reading, "Another Miraculous Catch," hints that this same thing happened before.

The first miraculous catch occurred when Jesus began his ministry and was looking for disciples to follow him (Luke 5:1–11). He uses Peter's boat as a pulpit to talk to a crowd.

When he finishes teaching, he tells Peter to head to deep water and let down his nets. Peter and his crew had fished all night and caught nothing. They're no doubt tired and discouraged. Yet when Jesus, who's a carpenter and not a fisherman, tells them to head out again, Peter agrees.

They catch so many fish that their nets are about to break, and their boats begin to sink. Peter bows before Jesus.

"Don't be afraid," Jesus says to him. "From now on you will fish for people." They pull their boats to shore and follow him. This is how Jesus begins his ministry and how it starts for the disciples.

Now the miracle happens a second time, this time as Jesus wraps up his earthly ministry. Both times it's a miracle. Both times he gets Peter's attention. It also serves as a reminder that Jesus wants Peter to fish for people.

Questions: *How well do we do at obeying God when his instructions make little sense? What has God done to get our attention?*

Prayer: Lord Jesus, may we obey you and follow your call on our lives.

DAY 27: JESUS FEEDS HIS DISCIPLES

TODAY'S PASSAGE: JOHN 21:7–14

Focus verse: *Then the disciple whom Jesus loved said to Peter, "It is the Lord!"* (John 21:7)

As Peter focuses on the large catch of fish, John looks toward the man on the shore and recognizes him. "It's the Lord!" he says to Peter.

As soon as Peter hears this, he jumps into the water and swims to the beach. His desire to get to Jesus as quickly as possible is a great impulse. But in doing so he leaves his fishing companions to deal with the fish and get the boat safely ashore.

When they arrive, Jesus already has a fire going

with fish cooking over burning coals. He doesn't need any of the fish his disciples just caught. He already has fish and is preparing them to eat. Jesus also has some bread waiting.

It's a breakfast of fish and bread.

Several verses in the Bible mention a meal of fish and bread. Two of them occur in today's passage. Three more happen when Jesus miraculously feeds over five thousand people. Starting with five loaves of bread and two fish, Jesus multiplies the food to feed all the people (Matthew 14:13–21, Mark 6:30–44, and Luke 9:10–17).

Another time, Jesus starts with seven loaves and a few small fish. (The text says loaves, and we assume it's loaves of bread.) This time he feeds over four thousand people (Matthew 15:29–39 and Mark 8:1–13).

Even though Jesus already has a meal prepared for them, he tells Peter to get some of the fish they caught. It's not clear why he says this, but John uses it to communicate two things. First is the precise number of fish caught. Knowing this detail tells us John was there. The other is that, despite a large catch which should have broken the nets, they didn't tear. This is another delightful detail of the miraculous catch.

Jesus invites his disciples to eat breakfast. Having fished all night, they've certainly built up an appetite. He takes the bread and distributes it to them, just like he did at the Passover meal a few weeks earlier when he instituted the practice of Holy Communion. He also passes out the fish.

Yet consider this meal.

Did Jesus take the time to buy bread, catch fish, find firewood, start a fire, and roast the fish? He could have. Or he could have miraculously made it all happen. If so, this becomes a third food miracle. He first multiplied food to feed five thousand people and later fed four thousand. This time, however, he may have started with nothing.

Regardless of how it happens, Jesus feeds his disciples.

But why does Jesus feed them? Though they're surely hungry, they also have a net full of fish. They could have fed themselves. Yet Jesus feeds them anyway, just because he can.

It's a reminder that sometimes God does things for us, just because.

Questions: *Is our impulse like Peter's, to get to Jesus as quickly as possible? When has God used a miracle to feed us* *or take care of us? When has Jesus done something for us just because?*

Prayer: Our Father in heaven, give us today our daily bread, just as Jesus instructed us to pray (Matthew 6:11 and Luke 11:3).

DAY 28: WORSHIP AND DOUBT
TODAY'S PASSAGE: MATTHEW 28:16–17

Focus verse: *When they saw him, they worshiped him; but some doubted.* (Matthew 28:17)

In Matthew's gospel of Jesus, he writes that Jesus tells Mary to instruct his followers to "Go to Galilee." A few verses later they do exactly that. But John doesn't mention Jesus telling them to go to Galilee or say when they travel there. We just know they're in Galilee for the great catch of fish (Day 26).

As a result, it's unclear where today's passage from Matthew best aligns with John's timeline. But because it fits thematically into our story arc at this point, we'll cover it now.

The eleven remaining disciples go to Galilee as Jesus instructed. They meet him there. When they see him, they worship him. But some have doubts plague them.

What might their worship look like? They may bow down before him.

They're certainly overjoyed to see him. Can wrapping their arms around him to give him a strong hug count as worship? I suspect so.

Though it may bother us to consider hugging Jesus as a form of worship, it's what's in our heart that matters—not what others think. When we worship, we must worship in the Spirit and in truth. These are the kind of worshipers the Father desires (John 4:23–24).

Part of worshiping God in truth may be to keep our focus on him and not distract ourselves with concern over the opinions of others. In God's eternal perspective, what others think or say about us doesn't matter. Only God's opinion counts.

Yet coupled with this phrase about worshiping him, Matthew notes that some doubt. He doesn't say that some worship and some doubt. The implication is that they all worship, even though some doubt.

Can we honestly worship God if we doubt? I think so. I hope so.

If we only worship God once we push all doubt aside, I suspect our worship of him would occur much less frequently—if at all.

We know God delights in our worship. I can imagine him delighting even more when we worship him in the face of our doubt. Though uncertainty may at times linger in our minds, we shove that aside to give our adoration to the Almighty, our Creator, and our Savior.

This may be the sweetest form of worship we can offer.

Questions: *How do we best worship God? When have we let doubts hinder our worship of him or our service for him?*

Prayer: Lord, may we worship you in the Spirit and in truth. And may we do so even more when doubt afflicts us.

DAY 29: JESUS RESTORES PETER
TODAY'S PASSAGE: JOHN 21:15–19

Focus verse: *Peter was hurt because Jesus asked him the third time, "Do you love me?"* (John 21:17)

Right before Jesus was crucified, he predicted that Peter would deny him three times. The confident disciple was adamant it wouldn't happen, that he was willing to go to prison and even die for Jesus (Matthew 26:31–35, Mark 14:27–31, Luke 22:31–34, and John 13:37–38).

Yet a few hours later Peter does exactly what Jesus said he would do. He denies knowing his Rabbi three times, with increasing fervor each time, confirming his final denial with an oath. This supplies a three-fold confirmation that he denies knowing Jesus (Matthew 26:69–75, Mark 14:66–72, Luke 22:54–62, and John 18:15–18, 25–27).

Peter must wallow in guilt over how quickly he gave in to fear and disavowed his master. Despite his self-assuredness, Peter is weak. His commitment to Jesus is fickle. His pledge to die for his master means nothing.

Though Peter's failure could cause him to give up, even to end his life like Judas did, he does not. He sticks around.

This is because of Jesus's prayer for his disciple. "I have prayed for you, Simon, that your faith may not fail. And when you have turned back, strengthen your brothers" (Luke 22:32).

Ever since Jesus rose from the dead, he's worked to bring Peter back into his fold. He first appears to Peter separately (see Day 21 and Luke 24:34) and then three more times when Peter is with other disciples (Days 22, 25, and 27). In doing so, Peter knows Jesus has forgiven him and includes him with the other disciples.

Now Jesus completes his disciple's restoration.

Three times Jesus has Peter affirm his master, with each affirmation offsetting a denial. It distresses Peter to have to affirm Jesus three times.

But consider how much more Jesus must have been distressed for his disciple to deny even knowing him.

Jesus's first question to Peter is pointed. "Do you love me more than these?" It's not enough for Peter to profess loving Jesus as much as the other disciples, who didn't deny him. Instead, he must profess a greater love. Peter does.

In response to each of Peter's three affirmations, Jesus tells Peter what to do. The first time he says, "Feed my lambs." A lamb is a baby sheep. The second time Jesus says, "Take care of my sheep." The third time the Savior says, "Feed my sheep."

Who are the sheep Peter is supposed to care for? Jesus's sheep are his followers, specifically his disciples. Recall that in Jesus's earlier prayer, he asked his Father that Peter, once restored, would strengthen the brothers.

Though this three-fold restoration sequence is painful for Peter, it's necessary.

Having now been restored, Jesus tells Peter what will happen when he gets old. Implicitly he'll be crucified, and his death will glorify God.

But until then, Jesus tells Peter the same thing he did at the start of their time together. "Follow me" (Matthew 4:18–19).

And following Jesus is what matters most.

Questions: *How well do we do at following Jesus today? Will we do so for the rest of our lives, regardless of what may happen?*

Prayer: Jesus, may we follow you and feed your sheep.

DAY 30: WHAT ABOUT JOHN?
TODAY'S PASSAGE: JOHN 21:20–23

Focus verse: *When Peter saw [John], he asked, "Lord, what about him?"* (John 21:21)

After restoring Peter into a right relationship with him, Jesus adds a cryptic line that implies Peter will die by crucifixion when he is older. This must make Peter squirm even more.

Looking around, Peter notices John trailing behind them, having heard the whole conversation. Peter tips his head toward his fellow disciple and asks Jesus, "What about him?"

We can speculate on Peter's motivation for asking this question.

It may be he's uncomfortable with all the attention Jesus is giving him, first by asking him three times to affirm his love and then telling him how he's going to die. Peter asks his question to shift the attention to John.

Or it might be Peter comparing himself to John. Will Peter suffer more for his Savior? If so, that could be a source of pride.

Perhaps Peter merely wants to know if the other disciple will endure the same fate as him. If so, it becomes an issue of fairness, a plague that grips many today, as in, "It's not fair!"

Regardless, Jesus says John's path doesn't matter as far as Peter is concerned. All he must do is follow Jesus and not worry about John.

Yet Jesus communicates this rhetorically, saying "If I want him to live until I return, what's it to you?"

Some disciples misunderstand Jesus. They assume he means John will not die. John sets the record straight for his readers and confirms that Jesus didn't say John wouldn't die.

We need to listen to what people say and not jump to false conclusions. And when unfounded rumors start, we should do what we can to stop them. When people spread false assumptions, even when their intentions are good, confusion is a sure result.

We can also learn an important lesson from Peter. Regardless of his reason for asking Jesus about John's future, the result would be Peter being able to compare himself to John.

Comparing ourselves with others accomplishes nothing positive. It can lead to unwarranted pride or cause harmful despair. Both extremes impede us from following Jesus and serving him. Instead, we should keep our focus on Jesus (Hebrews 12:1–2).

Jesus simply tells Peter, "You must follow me." And we must do the same.

Questions: *When have we made the mistake of comparing ourselves to others? Are we more likely to start a rumor, spread it, or stop it?*

Prayer: Jesus, show us how we can best follow you.

DAY 31: JOHN'S CONCLUSION

TODAY'S PASSAGE: JOHN 21:24–25, ALONG WITH JOHN 20:30–31

Focus verse: *These are written that you may believe that Jesus is the Messiah, the Son of God, and that by believing you may have life in his name.* (John 20:31)

After John writes that Jesus didn't say John wouldn't die, the disciple wraps up his biography of the Messiah. He confirms that he witnessed the things he wrote about and pledges that his testimony about Jesus is true.

And we have no reason to doubt John's veracity. As one of Jesus's twelve disciples and part of his inner circle of three, John was there to see firsthand what he writes about Jesus.

Yet John doesn't include everything in his gospel

account. There's even more. From his perspective two thousand years ago, the world could not contain all the books that would be required to fully document all Jesus said and did.

Today, we would not make this same claim. With ease people can write and publish books. And if they're in electronic form, they take up no space on a library shelf. They merely use storage space in a computer.

Even so, we can extend John's comment to apply to us today in a figurative sense. That is, the entire world is not big enough to contain the glorious magnitude of who Jesus is. Just as he lives outside our reality, his being also transcends it.

This isn't John's first conclusion to his writing. We need to go back one chapter to read it. It's easy to see John 20:30–31 being the end of the book, with chapter 21 serving as an epilogue. Therefore, it's not surprising that John gives us two conclusions, one to the main text of the book and the other to the epilogue.

In his first conclusion, John writes that Jesus performed many other signs before his disciples that the apostle didn't cover. This aligns with his second conclusion in chapter 21.

But there's more. And it's important, critically so.

What John writes, he did so that we might believe. And what does he want us to believe?

He wants us to believe that Jesus is the Messiah, that Jesus is the Son of God, and that by believing in him we may have life in his name.

Questions: *Do we believe Jesus is the Messiah, the son of God, and we have life through him? Who do we need to share this good news with?*

Prayer: Jesus, thank you for coming to earth to save us and giving us life in your name.

DAY 32: THE PROMISED HOLY SPIRIT
TODAY'S PASSAGE: LUKE 24:49 AND ACTS 1:4

Focus verse: *"I am going to send you what my Father has promised."* (Luke 24:49)

L uke wraps up his gospel by sharing Jesus's concluding words to his disciples. He starts by teaching them from Scripture about himself (see Day 23). He tells them he will send them what the Father promised. But he gives no more details about what this promise includes.

However, this isn't the first time he's talked about this promised gift with his disciples. He's already said it twice, so this should be a review for them. Both times happened before his crucifixion.

The first mention occurs among the teaching he gives them when they celebrate the Passover meal together, when he institutes Holy Communion. Jesus predicts his betrayal and Peter's denial, among many other things.

Sandwiched amid his lengthy teaching, Jesus tells his disciples he'll ask the Father to give them another advocate—the Holy Spirit—to help them and be with them forever (John 14:16).

Later in the evening, he tells them he's going away. They're distraught. To comfort them, Jesus says that unless he goes away, the Advocate cannot come. But after Jesus leaves, he'll send the Advocate to them (John 16:7).

In the Old Testament, Job acknowledges that his advocate, his witness, is in heaven (Job 16:19). Faced with unhelpful and hurtful feedback from his friends, Job looks to his advocate to vindicate him.

Another name for the Advocate is the Holy Spirit.

Though the Holy Spirit shows up in dramatic fashion in the book of Acts and guides Jesus's church through the rest of the New Testament, he's also present in the Old Testament. The name Spirit, with a capital S, appears throughout the Old

Testament Scripture. The more complete label of Holy Spirit also shows up, but not as often.

In one of his psalms, David implores God, "Do not cast me from your presence or take your Holy Spirit from me" (Psalm 51:11). And Isaiah asks plaintively, "Where is he who set his Holy Spirit among them?" (Isaiah 63:11).

In his future-focused prophecy, the prophet Joel envisions a future when God will pour out his Spirit on all people. They will prophesy, dream dreams, and see visions. This will be to everyone, both men and women. God's Spirit will reveal to them the wonders of heaven and of earth (Joel 2:28–30).

Jesus's disciples are no doubt familiar with Joel's prophetic words. What we don't know is if they connect the prophet's predictions with Jesus's promise.

Even if they don't see the connection, they will soon see this Old Testament prophecy fulfilled in the most spectacular way. And so will thousands of others.

Questions: *What role does the Holy Spirit play in our lives today? What other gifts has God promised to give us?*

Prayer: Holy Spirit, may you guide us in all that we do.

DAY 33: CONNECTING LUKE AND ACTS

TODAY'S PASSAGE: ACTS 1:1–3

Focus verse: *In my former book, Theophilus, I wrote about all that Jesus began to do and to teach.* (Acts 1:1)

We've wrapped up the book of John, using it as the basis for our story arc up to this point. Now we'll switch our focus to the first two chapters in the book of Acts, tapping it to guide our remaining discussions.

Doctor Luke wrote Acts. He also wrote the Gospel of Luke, which is named after him. Luke's writings combine to provide us with a compelling history of Jesus and his church. As such, we should carefully consider what he says.

Luke researched and wrote both his books for

Theophilus, a man Scripture tells us little about. What we do know is that Luke wanted Theophilus to know for sure what he had been taught about Jesus (Luke 1:3–4). Luke continues his mission in the book of Acts to assure Theophilus—and all who read his writing, including us.

Luke's two books overlap a bit. He opens Acts with a concise review of the end of Jesus's life from the Gospel of Luke, and then he foreshadows some events he will soon cover—and which we'll soon cover.

In the book of Luke, the doctor shares what Jesus did and taught while on earth and until he ascended into heaven. We'll explore this on Day 40.

On that eventful day, Jesus will instruct his chosen followers through the Holy Spirit. Prior to that, he suffered—that is, died on the cross for our sins—and rose from the dead. He appeared to his followers multiple times over the course of forty days, teaching them about the kingdom of God.

Luke, however, doesn't share any of Jesus's teaching about the kingdom of God here in Acts. But he—and the other gospel writers—covers the topic extensively prior to Jesus's death. Altogether, *kingdom of God* appears in over fifty verses in the four gospels. (Matthew's preferred label, *kingdom of heaven*, shows up thirty-one times.)

Here are four of the things Jesus says about the kingdom of God, one from each gospel writer:

"Therefore I tell you that the kingdom of God will be taken away from you and given to a people who will produce its fruit" (Matthew 21:43).

"Let the little children come to me, and do not hinder them, for the kingdom of God belongs to such as these" (Mark 10:14).

"People will come from east and west and north and south, and will take their places at the feast in the kingdom of God" (Luke 13:29).

"Very truly I tell you, no one can see the kingdom of God unless they are born again" (John 3:3).

Questions: *What does the kingdom of God mean to you? How do you fit into the kingdom of God?*

Prayer: Father God, show us how we can best advance your kingdom.

DAY 34: WAIT IN JERUSALEM

TODAY'S PASSAGE: ACTS 1:4–5, ALONG WITH LUKE 24:49

Focus verse: *"John baptized with water, but in a few days you will be baptized with the Holy Spirit."* (Acts 1:5)

After Luke concludes his introduction to the book of Acts, straightaway he shares a story about Jesus and his disciples. And he quotes Jesus. Though we think of the words of Jesus as appearing only in the four gospel accounts —Matthew, Mark, Luke, and John—our Savior's words also appear in the book of Acts (as well as 2 Corinthians and Revelation).

Jesus instructs his followers to not leave Jerusalem, but to wait there to receive the Father's promised gift, which Jesus has already told them about (Day 32). In his gospel, Luke confirms this, writing that Jesus tells his disciples to "stay in the city." This means they're already in Jerusalem.

As you may recall, the last time we knew where the disciples were was in Day 26 when they were in Galilee, specifically the Sea of Galilee for the great catch of fish. And we covered Jesus's instructions to go there in Day 14.

This change in location back to Jerusalem isn't trivial. It's seventy miles away (113 kilometers) and would take three to four days to walk.

Just as we don't know exactly when they left Jerusalem to go to Galilee, we also don't know when they returned. But at this point in our story, they're in Jerusalem, and Jesus tells them to wait there.

Next Jesus explains what will happen more fully. "Though John baptized with water, in a few days you'll be baptized with the Holy Spirit."

Water baptism signifies repentance, while Holy Spirit baptism signifies God's Spirit coming to live in us, something all people experience—to varying degrees—after they believe in Jesus.

John the baptizer also mentions Holy Spirit baptism through Jesus in Mark 1:8. More pointedly, Matthew and Luke write that John the Baptist says

Jesus will baptize the people with "the Holy Spirit and fire" (Matthew 3:11 and Luke 3:16).

What does baptism by the Holy Spirit and fire mean?

We can think of fire as a means of judgment, as well as purification.

The prophet Malachi foresaw this when he asks, "Who can stand before him? He will be like a refiner's fire or a launderer's soap. He will refine and purify" (see Malachi 3:2–5).

For those who follow Jesus, he will purify them through the refiner's fire. Those who don't follow him will face the fire of judgment.

Questions: *How well do we react when our Lord tells us to wait? What does baptism with the Holy Spirit and fire mean to you?*

Prayer: Lord Jesus, thank you for baptizing us with the Holy Spirit and fire, purifying us and preparing us to advance the kingdom of God.

DAY 35: WHEN WILL IT HAPPEN?

TODAY'S PASSAGE: ACTS 1:6–7

Focus verse: *Then [the disciples] gathered around him and asked him, "Lord, are you at this time going to restore the kingdom to Israel?"* (Acts 1:6)

Jesus told his disciples that in a few days the Holy Spirit will baptize them. Yet he doesn't offer any clarification on what this means, and they don't ask him to explain. If it were me, I'd want to know more. With questions swirling in my mind, I'd want details.

But the disciples don't seek answers. Instead, as if they didn't even hear him mention Holy Spirit baptism, they ask him something else.

"Are you going to restore the kingdom of Israel now?"

I groan when I hear this. I imagine the Messiah groaning as well.

The disciples still don't seem to understand why Jesus came to earth. He's not here to lead a military rebellion. His plan isn't—and never was—to fight against the Roman regime that occupies his people's land and threatens their existence.

Yet this is what the disciples expect.

Though their misinterpretation of Old Testament prophecy—and the common expectation of most of their people—supports their perspective, Jesus's teaching doesn't. Jesus didn't come to rescue them physically but to save them spiritually.

And his disciples still don't get it.

With all the miracles Jesus performed, along with him rising from the dead, the disciples may assume he can do anything. From a man who controlled the demons, healed people, and raised the dead, amassing an army and overthrowing their Roman oppressors is a reasonable conclusion.

There's no doubt in my mind Jesus could do that—if that's what he wanted to do. But that isn't his mission. His mission is spiritual liberation from the bondage of sin, not the bondage of an occupying force.

Jesus could have used their rash question to expose their misunderstanding as a teachable moment, but he doesn't.

This might be because he knows that in a few days the disciples will, in fact, undergo Holy Spirit baptism. And when the Advocate comes, he'll teach them all things and remind them of everything Jesus said (John 14:26). After this occurs, Jesus's teaching about why he came to earth will become apparent.

Through the Holy Spirit, they will finally understand.

Questions: *When have we had wrong expectations of Jesus? Do we believe the Holy Spirit can teach us all things?*

Prayer: Holy Spirit, teach us what we need to know and remind us about Jesus.

DAY 36: THE GREAT COMMISSION
TODAY'S PASSAGE: MATTHEW 28:18–20

Focus verse: *"Go and make disciples of all nations."*
(Matthew 28:19)

As Jesus prepares to return to heaven, he has one final bit of instruction for his disciples. He commissions them to continue what he started and tell others the good news about how he died in their place to save them from their sins.

The Bible records these final instructions in three places—here in Matthew, as well as in Mark and Acts. Each differs from the others. We'll cover each one in turn in our next three readings.

The most common one occurs in Matthew's biography of Jesus. Over the years I've heard many preachers speak on this passage. It's often called the Great Commission. It's great because no other commissioning charge is more important than telling the world about Jesus.

Jesus begins by saying that all authority in heaven and on earth belongs to him. Implicitly he imparts this authority to his followers. Based on this he tells them to go and make disciples—everywhere.

He doesn't tell them to make converts. He tells them to make disciples. Contrary to how most churches behave today, converts—or new members —isn't the goal. Disciples are what matters to Jesus. If it matters to Jesus, it should matter to us.

Jesus also tells them to go to all nations. Two thousand years ago most Jews assumed the promised Savior was coming for their nation only and no others. Yet a careful reading of the Old Testament reveals that God planned all along that Jesus would save Gentiles, too, not just the Jews. The Scriptures allude to this multiple times.

As Jesus's followers go and make disciples, they're to do two things: baptize and teach.

Baptism is a public testimony of aligning with Jesus. Most of his followers today make much about baptism, arguing over how it should occur and what it means. In considering these issues, we must remember the rebel crucified next to Jesus. Jesus promised him salvation based on his verbal assent, and he was never baptized. Though baptism is important, the meaning behind it is even more important. Hold on to this truth.

The other thing the disciples are to do is teach. Jesus wants them to teach people to obey everything he commanded them to do. But the people are supposed to obey Jesus's commands, not the Old Testament ones. This is a key distinction.

Jesus commanded little of us. We're supposed to follow and believe in him (Matthew 16:24 and John 11:25). Next, we are to love God and love others (Matthew 22:37–40, Luke 10:27, and 1 John 3:23). If we do these things, we'll be in great shape.

Jesus concludes by saying that he'll be with us always, even to the end of time. And he'll do this through the Holy Spirit who will arrive in a few days.

Questions: *What should our response be to Jesus's final instructions to his followers? What are we doing to obey Jesus's essential command to make disciples?*

Prayer: Jesus, wherever we go may we tell others about you and make disciples.

DAY 37: THESE SIGNS

TODAY'S PASSAGE: MARK 16:15–18

Focus verse: *"And these signs will accompany those who believe . . ."* (Mark 16:17)

Mark also records Jesus's parting remarks to his disciples. This passage is not well known. It's mostly ignored. I don't recall ever hearing a sermon about it. The likely reason is that Jesus's final instructions to his followers ends with a list of signs that those who believe in him will have. It's a list that confounds many people today. Therefore, it's easier to ignore it than to believe it.

Like Matthew's version, Mark writes that Jesus

tells his followers to go throughout the world and preach the gospel, baptizing those who believe. Those who believe will be saved, but those who don't believe will be condemned.

Jesus then lists five traits that those who believe in him will have.

First, they will drive out demons. Regardless of how we perceive demons or the way they manifest their afflictions on people today, as followers of Jesus, we'll drive out demons.

Next, Jesus's followers will speak in tongues. We don't know if this means they'll speak in human languages they don't know to others or in spiritual languages to God. But regardless, they'll speak in tongues. We'll see Peter do this in Day 47 when he addresses people in their native languages at Pentecost. And Paul teaches about the other type of tongues in 1 Corinthians 14:5–6.

Third, they will pick up snakes with their hands. Implicitly, the serpents won't hurt them. This happened to Paul on the island of Malta (Acts 28:3–5).

Fourth, they'll drink deadly poison, but it won't hurt them at all.

Last, they'll lay their hands on sick people and heal them.

This list gives me pause, as it does for many followers of Jesus. Though I believe each one of these items is possible, I've only had personal experience with the fifth one, of using Jesus's authority to heal people. And this doesn't occur as often as I'd like.

Personally, I want to stay as far away as possible from snakes and poison. Yet I have confidence that if I inadvertently encounter either, Jesus will protect me. As far as driving out demons and speaking in tongues, I'm open to both. But so far, I haven't experienced either.

Like me, most people have varying degrees of acceptance and revulsion over these five items that Jesus says *all* who believe in him will possess. The easy response is to ignore these words, and pretend Jesus never said them. But he did.

Therefore, we should consider them, too, even if it takes a lifetime to do so.

Questions: *What is your response to these five items? What can you do to seek a better understanding of this passage that confounds many?*

Prayer: Holy Spirit, teach us what this passage means and how we should best live it out.

DAY 38: MY WITNESSES

TODAY'S PASSAGE: ACTS 1:8 AND ALSO LUKE 24:48

Focus verse: *"You will be my witnesses in Jerusalem, and in all Judea and Samaria, and to the ends of the earth."* (Acts 1:8)

Compared to Matthew and Mark, Luke writes the least about Jesus's final words to his disciples before he ascends into heaven. And this is despite Luke covering this event in both his books: at the end of Luke and the start of Acts.

In the book of Luke, he writes that Jesus opens their minds so they can understand the Scriptures (see Day 23). He reminds them he came to die for them and rise from the dead to forgive all who repent. They're to tell everyone throughout the world, starting in Jerusalem (Luke 24:45–47).

After that, Luke notes that Jesus simply says, "You will be my witnesses of these things." But first they need to wait for the Holy Spirit (Day 32 and Day 34). Once they receive Holy Spirit power, they can move forward as Jesus's witnesses to tell others who he is and what he did.

In the slightly expanded version in the book of Acts, Jesus says that his disciples will receive power when the Holy Spirit comes upon them. Then they can be his witnesses in Jerusalem, Judea, Samaria, and the ends of the earth.

This list of geographies carries significance to both them and to us today.

Jerusalem is the town where the disciples are. It's not where they're from, as most came from Galilee. But they're in Jerusalem now. And Jerusalem is the center of Jewish worship. Strategically, this is the ideal place for the disciples to begin telling others about Jesus. First, they're already there. Second, it's their people's religious center.

Next is Judea. Judea isn't a town but a region. It's the area surrounding Jerusalem. It's effectively the space once occupied by the nation of Judah, after it separated from the rest of Israel. This is where many of the Jews live. Because of Roman occupation, Judea is no longer a country, but it mentally serves as one for the Jewish people. When Jesus tells his disciples to go into Judea, he's effectively telling them to witness in their own country, to their own people.

The third area on Jesus's list is Samaria. You may recall Jesus's interaction with the Samaritan woman at the well (John 4:1–26) or his parable about the Good Samaritan (Luke 10:25–37). Both underscore the fact that the Jews and Samaritans didn't get along with each other and that the Jews looked down on the Samaritans as inferior.

Yet Jesus treated Samaritans well. He wants his disciples to be his witnesses to them, even though culturally and religiously they're to avoid any interactions with these people. Jesus modeled that this distinction doesn't matter to him, and it shouldn't to his disciples. He wants them to go there.

The last item on Jesus's list covers everything else. It's to the "ends of the earth." This means the rest of the world.

When we think about sending missionaries to witness for Jesus, this is the geography we first think about. And though we shouldn't dismiss people in other countries, let's not lose sight of being his witness where we live now, to our own country, and to the people living near us whom society rejects.

Questions: *Who should we witness to? Though not everyone can go to another country to tell them about Jesus, how can we help those who do go?*

Prayer: Father God, show us how we can best tell others about Jesus.

DAY 39: THE TEN APPEARANCES OF JESUS

TODAY'S PASSAGE: 1 CORINTHIANS 15:3–8

Focus verse: *After that, he appeared to more than five hundred of the brothers and sisters at the same time, most of whom are still living . . . Then he appeared to James.*
(1 Corinthians 15:6–7)

As we move along from Jesus's resurrection to his ascension into heaven, we've covered many of the people Jesus revealed himself to. It's important to have this list of eyewitness accounts who can confirm that Jesus did, in fact, rise from the dead.

Here are the ten appearances of Jesus that Scripture records for us. These people all offer testimony that Jesus rose from the dead:

1. Jesus first appears to Mary Magdalene. We covered this in Day 13.

2. Next, Jesus shows himself to Simon Peter. We covered this in Day 21.

3. Around this same time Jesus reveals himself to Cleopas and his friend as they travel to Emmaus. We covered this in Days 15 through 21.

4. Later that evening, Jesus appears to ten of the disciples (Day 22).

5. A week after that, Jesus shows himself to Thomas, along with the other ten disciples (Day 25).

6. Later, at the Sea of Galilee, Jesus reveals himself to seven disciples: Simon Peter, Thomas, Nathaniel, James, John, and two others (Day 26).

7. Just before Jesus ascends into heaven, all his disciples are there when he tells them to share the good news with others (Days 36, 37, and 38).

8. Though Matthew, Mark, Luke, and John don't mention it in their accounts of Jesus, Paul says Jesus appears to over five hundred people, most of whom are

still alive when Paul writes his letter
(1 Corinthians 15:6).

9. And Jesus appears to James. We didn't
    mention this in our readings because
    none of the gospel writers cover this. But
    Paul does. Paul writes that Jesus appears
    individually to James (1 Corinthians
    15:7). Though this could be the disciple
    James (John's brother), it's more likely
    Paul means James, the brother of Jesus.

10. But there's one more person Jesus
    appears to. It's Paul. But this doesn't
    happen until *after* Jesus ascends into
    heaven (Acts 9:1–6).

Jesus's subsequent appearance to Paul repre-
sents everyone the Messiah has shown himself to
over the centuries. And what an amazing testimony
they have.

Questions: *Though Jesus doesn't appear to most people,
how has he revealed himself to you? What is your testimony
about Jesus?*

Prayer: Thank you, Jesus, for revealing yourself to us through Scripture, the Holy Spirit, and sometimes even in person.

DAY 40: JESUS ASCENDS INTO HEAVEN

TODAY'S PASSAGE: ACTS 1:9, ALONG WITH
MARK 16:19 AND LUKE 24:50–52

Focus verse: *He was taken up before their very eyes, and a cloud hid him from their sight.* (Acts 1:9)

After Jesus gives his parting instructions to his disciples and commissions them to be his witnesses throughout the entire world, he has completed all he came to earth to do. It's time for him to leave. It's time for him to return to his Father in heaven.

In the book of Acts, Luke records this succinctly. After Jesus instructs them, he's taken up into the sky as they watch. A cloud covers him. That's it.

Mark is also brief. He simply writes that Jesus is taken up into heaven to sit at God's right hand.

Perhaps the reason Luke doesn't provide any detail about this in the book of Acts, is that he already did so in his biography of Jesus. In Luke he writes that Jesus took his disciples to a place near Bethany. He lifts his hands to bless them. Though I'd really like to know what his blessing was, Luke doesn't tell us. But I'm sure it was an amazing one.

As he blesses them, his body levitates. He rises upward. He ascends into heaven.

Consider what the disciples have gone through in the past forty days. It's been a roller coaster of emotions for them, one we can scarcely comprehend.

The man they followed and committed their lives to was killed on a cross. Forgetting that he said he would rise from the dead, they fall into deep despair. It's all over. Everything they dreamed of and hoped to happen is gone. Their lives are in disarray and their future is a huge question mark.

Then they hear an incredible report that Jesus has risen from the dead, that he's alive. Hope stirs within. Soon after that, Jesus appears to them, confirming his resurrection. Their emotions soar.

However, it's not long before he tells them he's leaving them again, this time for good. Their hope sags. How could their Rabbi abandon them and not be there to guide them?

But this is a good thing for him to go away, he says. Unless he leaves, until he leaves, the promised comforter, the Advocate, the Holy Spirit, cannot arrive. They take solace in this, even if they don't like the idea of Jesus going away. I'm sure they're emotionally torn.

As he prepares to leave, Jesus gives a final bit of encouragement. He teaches them, just like always, but now they understand. At that his body rises into heaven. And he's gone.

What are they thinking at this point? They could be sad that he's left or excited over the gift he promised to send them: the Holy Spirit.

Regardless, they worship him and return to Jerusalem filled with joy.

Questions: *When the unexpected occurs, do we wallow in despair or anticipate what God will do next? Would we rather have Jesus with us or the Holy Spirit in us?*

Prayer: May we worship you, Jesus, for what you did, and may we embrace you, Holy Spirit, for what you are doing in our lives.

DAY 41: AFTER JESUS ASCENDS

TODAY'S PASSAGE: ACTS 1:10–11

Focus verse: *"Men of Galilee," they said, "why do you stand here looking into the sky?"* (Acts 1:11)

As we covered yesterday in the book of Acts, Luke merely writes that after Jesus taught his disciples he was taken up as they watched, and a cloud hid him from them.

I doubt they've ever seen anyone ascend into heaven. I doubt anyone has. Imagine their eyes fixated on the spot where they last saw him. Even though he clearly told them he must leave before the Holy Spirit can come, I wonder if they're holding their breath, secretly hoping to see him reappear in the sky and descend back to earth.

They've certainly seen many perplexing things during their time with Jesus, so it wouldn't surprise them to see him come back right away in the same way he left.

As they stare up into the sky, suddenly two men dressed in white appear beside them. Luke uses similar wording to describe what the women saw at Jesus's open tomb (Luke 24:4). Yet John directly says these two men in white at the tomb are, in fact, angels (Day 1). Therefore, the two men in white that Luke writes about here are likely angels too.

I can't find any other place in Scripture where God dispatches two angels to communicate truth to his people. Yet two angels show up at both Jesus's resurrection and his ascension. This highlights how important these two events are in the lives of those who follow Jesus. First, he rises from the dead to prove his mastery over death. Then he ascends into heaven so the Holy Spirit can come to us.

Both times, two angels serve as witnesses. They underscore the importance of Jesus's resurrection and ascension. These stand as essential cornerstones of our faith.

This time, the angels ask why the disciples stare into the sky. "Jesus, the one you watched ascend into heaven," the heavenly messengers say, "will one day return in the same way."

Jesus had already told them he would one day come back to get them so they could live with him (John 14:3). Paul will later confirm this in his first letter to the church in Thessalonica (1 Thessalonians 4:16–17).

The disciples' reaction also teaches us an important lesson.

Their upward gaze at where Jesus once was shows they're fixating on the past. Jesus just told them about the future and what they're supposed to do. But they're not doing it—at least not yet.

Questions: *How often do we focus on what was and forget about what we're supposed to do? What has God told us to do that we're not yet doing?*

Prayer: Almighty God, we praise you for what you've done and look forward to what you will do. May we rightly balance the past, the present, and the future.

DAY 42: GATHERED IN PRAYER

TODAY'S PASSAGE: ACTS 1:12–15

Focus verse: *They all joined together constantly in prayer.*
(Acts 1:14)

No doubt jarred back to reality by the angels' question about why they're staring into space, the disciples return to Jerusalem. Jesus had told them to go there and wait for the gift the Father promised to send them, the present that couldn't arrive until after Jesus left. He told them to wait in Jerusalem, and that's exactly where they head.

Though Luke notes it's a Sabbath day's walk for them, it's not the Sabbath. Luke uses this description to let us know it's a short trip, one that won't take long.

When they arrive, they return upstairs to the room where they were staying. This is likely the same room they've been meeting in since Jesus rose from the dead. It may even be the same place where they celebrated Passover with their Rabbi. Both Mark and Luke say it's a large room.

Regardless, Luke lists the eleven disciples who are present. They are Peter, John, James, Andrew, Philip, Thomas, Bartholomew, Matthew, James son of Alphaeus, Simon the Zealot, and Judas son of James, not to be confused with Judas Iscariot who betrayed Jesus and is now dead.

These eleven disciples are the core group Jesus entrusted his ministry to. They're the ones who will go and make disciples, they are to teach and to baptize. Yet they're not alone. Others are there too.

Jesus's mother Mary is present, "along with the women." Though Luke doesn't say who they are, we can piece together a likely list based on those at his crucifixion and empty tomb as recorded by Matthew, Mark, Luke, and John in their gospel accounts of Jesus. This would include Mary Magdalene, the other Mary, Mary the mother of

James the younger and of Joseph, Salome, Joanna, Mary the wife of Clopas, Jesus's aunt, "and others."

But there are even more in the upper room. Jesus's brothers are there too. The last we heard about them, John writes that Jesus's own brothers did not believe in him (John 7:5). It seems they now do. Rising from the dead would certainly get their attention. Jesus has four brothers. They're James, Joseph, Simon, and Judas (Matthew 13:55 and Mark 6:3). And if Jesus's mother and brothers are there, it's likely his sisters are too (Matthew 13:56).

Based on this, we can speculate there were at least twenty people present. Yet there are many more. Luke says 120. Already the number of Jesus's followers has grown from twelve to 120, a tenfold increase in just a few weeks. And the Holy Spirit hasn't even yet arrived. Imagine what will happen when he does.

As they wait, they join in constant prayer. They're not passively doing nothing until the Holy Spirit shows up; they're praying. Prayer is a wise action as we wait on God.

Questions: *What is our default reaction when God wants* *us to wait? What situations are most likely to prompt us to pray?*

Prayer: Father God, when you want us to wait, show us the best way to do so.

DAY 43: REPLACING JUDAS

TODAY'S PASSAGE: ACTS 1:15–20

Focus verse: *"Scripture had to be fulfilled in which the Holy Spirit spoke long ago through David concerning Judas, who served as guide for those who arrested Jesus."* (Acts 1:16)

B esides praying, the disciples also do something else as they wait for the Holy Spirit. Peter takes the lead. The disciples may already accept him as their leader. He was in Jesus's inner circle. Peter was also often the first disciple to speak, whether good or bad. Yet Jesus also called Peter into leadership when he told Peter to "feed my sheep" (Day 29).

With 120 of Jesus's followers gathered, Peter

stands to address them. He mentions Judas, one of their own, one of the twelve disciples Jesus hand-picked to follow him. Peter reminds them that Judas betrayed Jesus.

Judas is dead and Luke parenthetically fills in the details. Judas used the money he received for betraying Jesus to buy a field. He went there and fell headlong into it, thereby killing himself. Implicitly, he died by suicide. The locals call it the Field of Blood.

This account, however, differs from Matthew's more concise explanation of Judas's demise. Matthew simply writes that, filled with remorse, Judas goes and hangs himself (Matthew 27:1–10). Regardless of the supporting details, Judas is dead. Jesus's original twelve disciples now number only eleven. Citing Old Testament prophecy, Peter wants to replace Judas and bring their number back to twelve.

The disciple quotes from two psalms, both written by King David several centuries earlier.

The first one says, "May his place be deserted; let there be no one to dwell in it" (from Psalm 69:25). David's first focus in penning this psalm is against his own enemies. Yet the future-focused prophecy aspect of it looks at Jesus's enemies, in this case Judas. Let no one live there, in the place called "Field of Blood."

David's second psalm says, "May another take his place of leadership" (from Psalm 109:8). As with the first passage, David's immediate focus is on his own tormentors, while the secondary meaning looks at Jesus's.

In citing these two passages from Scripture, it's unlikely Peter has the scrolls available for him to consult. He quotes them from memory.

In doing so, he uses Old Testament prophecy to inform their situation and direct their action. They need to replace Judas.

Questions: *Without having the written text to consult, how much of Scripture could we quote from memory? How should we use the Bible to best guide us today?*

Prayer: Father, may we hide your word in our heart (Psalm 119:11).

DAY 44: DRAWING LOTS

TODAY'S PASSAGE: ACTS 1:21–26

Focus verse: *"Show us which of these two you have chosen to take over this apostolic ministry, which Judas left to go where he belongs."* (Acts 1:24–25)

After Peter quotes these two passages from Psalms, he moves directly to make his point. He wants to replace Judas. Peter doesn't just recommend it. He says it's necessary.

As criteria for Judas's successor, Peter says it should be a man who was with Jesus the whole time, starting from Jesus's baptism by John up to Jesus's ascension into heaven. The person must also be a witness to Jesus's resurrection from the dead.

Personally, I'm disappointed Peter specifies they need to appoint a man. From my perspective, Mary Magdalene would be an excellent choice. And Jesus already tapped her to be a witness for him, so, implicitly, he approves. Yet from a practical standpoint, Mary's gender would work against her in that day's society at each turn. This would frustrate her and diminish her effectiveness. It's not fair, but it is a reality. May we do better today.

Remember that the group has already been in prayer. They're poised to move forward. They nominate two men who best meet the criteria Peter proposed. These are Barsabbas and Matthias. But the people don't vote as we might today. Instead, they pray that God will direct the outcome based on his knowledge of everyone's hearts. Then they cast lots.

The lot falls to Matthias. He is the new disciple to replace Judas. Once again, there are twelve.

Interestingly, despite Matthias becoming a disciple, it seems he fails to make much of his opportunity, for we never hear of him again in the Bible. Alternately, Barsabbas could have faced a tremendous disappointment. God did not choose him. He could have left in a huff, yet he sticks around. Later

Paul and Barnabas pick Barsabbas to go with them to Antioch (Acts 15:22).

This idea of casting lots to pick a leader may seem strange to us today, out of place, and even inappropriate. Essentially, they resort to a game of chance—gambling, if you will—to pick Judas's replacement. Yet they also ask God to direct the results. And by faith, they trust him with the outcome.

Though we could follow this process today, we need not feel obligated to do so. Luke describes what the church did, but there is no command to do that. Indeed, we don't see casting lots to choose a leader again in the rest of the New Testament.

The text is descriptive but not prescriptive. This is a distinction we should make as we read and study the Bible. Is the text merely describing what happened or is it telling us what we need to do? Without having this principle to guide us, we risk making wrong conclusions from what we read in the Bible. May we not make that error.

Questions: *What do you think about casting lots to pick church leaders? Are we comfortable to do so in faith, knowing that God can—and will—direct the outcome?*

Prayer: Holy Spirit, guide our thoughts as we study Scripture so that we may reach God-honoring conclusions.

DAY 45: THE HOLY SPIRIT COMES
TODAY'S PASSAGE: ACTS 2:1–4

Focus verse: *All of them were filled with the Holy Spirit and began to speak in other tongues as the Spirit enabled them.* (Acts 2:4)

Before Jesus ascended into heaven, he told his disciples to go to Jerusalem and wait for the gift the Father would send. He doesn't tell them how long they need to wait. Is it a few days, a few weeks, a few months?

They've now been waiting for ten days. Will it be much longer? They don't know. But if they're concerned, the Bible doesn't mention it.

Then, at the fiftieth day after Jesus's death and the tenth day after his ascension into heaven,

Pentecost occurs. The sound of a violent wind fills the house where they're staying. They see something that looks like fire descend upon them. The flames separate, with one tongue of fire coming to rest on top of each person.

The Holy Spirit fills them, and they speak in other languages. This is the first Pentecost, represented by God sending tongues of fire to his people.

In the Old Testament, God also sent fire when Solomon dedicated the temple to the Lord. The fire consumed the burnt offering and sacrifices. God's glory filled the place (2 Chronicles 7:1–3).

As God sent his fire to dedicate his temple, he now sends his fire on Pentecost to dedicate his people.

The word *Pentecost* only occurs three times in the Bible. This New Testament word doesn't appear at all in the Old Testament. *Pentecost* is a Greek word. It means fifty days. Pentecost first occurred fifty days after Jesus's death, which was after Jesus instituted the first Communion, and happened on Passover.

The Festival of Weeks (Leviticus 23:15–22 and Exodus 34:22) is an Old Testament term and doesn't show up in the New Testament. According to nonbiblical sources, the Festival of Weeks is also known as the Feast of Weeks, the Feast of Fifty Days, or Shavuot.

Shavuot celebrates the day Moses descended from the mountain with the Ten Commandments and the Law of God, the Torah. This happened fifty days after the first Passover. On this day, God gave his people the Law, which are the rules to guide their behavior.

In the New Testament, fifty days after the first Communion (which occurred on Passover), God gives his people the Holy Spirit—his indwelling presence to guide them in following him.

The parallelism is significant: In the Old Testament, we have the first Passover, followed fifty days later with Shavuot and the Law. In the New Testament, we have the first Communion, followed fifty days later with Pentecost and the Holy Spirit.

Also consider that, in the Old Testament, God gives his people the Law through Moses. In the New Testament, God sends his people the Holy Spirit through Jesus.

The Holy Spirit filled Jesus's followers two thousand years ago, just as he fills us today.

Questions: *Which of these Old Testament connections resonates with you the most? How is the Holy Spirit at work in your life?*

Prayer: Holy Spirit, thank you for coming to earth to fill Jesus's followers with your supernatural power. May we embrace your work in us today.

DAY 46: JEWS FROM EVERY NATION
TODAY'S PASSAGE: ACTS 2:5–12

Focus verse: *Amazed and perplexed, they asked one another, "What does this mean?"* (Acts 2:12)

The Holy Spirit has come upon the 120 people in the room where they were staying. Though it's speculation, this may be the upper room where Jesus and his disciples celebrated Passover, and he instituted the first Communion.

The noise of the rushing wind gets the attention of other people in Jerusalem. They hear the sound and wonder where it's coming from. They move toward the source of the disturbance. What they discover perplexes them even more. When they get to the house where Jesus's followers are filled with the Holy Spirit, the people hear words in their own language.

Though the disciples were in a large room when the Holy Spirit came to them, this room surely can't accommodate all those curious people who show up. I envision Peter and some others going to the house's balcony to address the throng who has arrived. As we'll soon learn, there are thousands.

There's the sound of rushing wind, tongues of fire, and people speaking in other languages. These are known languages, just not known to the disciples speaking them. Remember that Jesus said his followers would speak in new tongues (Mark 16:17).

Luke says there are many God-fearing Jews in Jerusalem. They come from every nation. They may have gathered to celebrate Shavuot. Thousands of these Jewish visitors, religious pilgrims to Jerusalem, converge to investigate the source of the noise and hear words spoken in their own language.

And when they will later leave Jerusalem to return home, they'll take this experience with them. They'll surely tell many others back home what happened and what they heard.

Luke lists over a dozen places where these people—both Jews and converts to Judaism—hail from. This list mentions Cyrene. Does the city sound familiar? Remember Simon of Cyrene? The Roman soldiers forced Simon to carry Jesus's cross to his execution.

I wonder if Simon of Cyrene is in Jerusalem for this occasion. After all, he was there for Passover, fifty days earlier. He may have stayed. Or he could have left and later returned.

If Simon is there, what a wonderful realization would hit him. Though soldiers forced him to carry Jesus's cross, and he played an unwilling part in an innocent man's execution, Simon could see the results of Jesus's death.

This would give him an opportunity to believe in Jesus and be baptized.

Questions: *Though you may have never heard a supernatural wind or seen tongues of fire, how has God gotten your attention? How do you react when you think about Pentecost?*

Prayer: Heavenly Father, thank you for sending the Holy Spirit to us on Pentecost. May we hear what he has to say and obey.

DAY 47: JOEL'S PROPHECY
TODAY'S PASSAGE: ACTS 2:13–24

Focus verse: *"This is what was spoken by the prophet Joel."* (Acts 2:16)

The throng flocks to the source of the commotion and hears their own language spoken. Though some are amazed, and others are perplexed, a third group mocks the disciples as nothing more than drunks.

Peter and the other disciples stand. Again, serving as their leader, Peter addresses all those who have gathered. "These people are not drunk," Peter says. "It's only nine in the morning!"

He asks their permission to let him explain. He

implores them to listen carefully. Then he quotes from the prophet Joel.

Though written centuries earlier, Joel looks forward to a time when God says he will pour out his Spirit on all people. They will prophesy, see visions, and dream dreams. Both men and women. He will show wonders in the heavens and signs on the earth (Joel 2:28–32, which Peter quotes in Acts 2:16–21).

Joel wraps up this passage by saying that everyone who calls on the name of the Lord will be saved (Joel 2:32 and Acts 2:21).

Through this Old Testament passage, Peter explains the disciples' behavior to the crowd. God's Holy Spirit is upon them, and they're prophesying. The Holy Spirit controls them, not wine.

After quoting Joel, Peter moves the people's attention to Jesus.

"Jesus was a man, sent from God. He performed miracles, signs, and wonders," Peter says. "Jesus was handed over to you Jews according to God's plan and foreknowledge. And you, along with the Romans, executed him on the cross, but God raised him from the dead, freeing him from death."

It's interesting that Peter lumps the Jews

together, implicating them all in Jesus's unjust death, when it was only a few members of the religious leadership that orchestrated this and brought it to be.

Suggesting that this is something all Jews had a hand in is incorrect. Or is it?

After all, everyone sins and falls short of reaching God's splendor (Romans 3:22–24). This means we all played a role in bringing about Jesus's sacrificial death. We all need Jesus to save us, both Jews and Gentiles. This means both the Jews two thousand years ago, and everyone who's ever lived since.

Questions: *How should we react knowing that we each played a role in bringing about Jesus's death? What do we think about Joel's prophecy that God's Spirit would come upon his people?*

Prayer: Jesus, though we're responsible in bringing about your death, may we not wallow in guilt but celebrate your solution that provides our salvation.

DAY 48: DAVID'S PROPHECY
TODAY'S PASSAGE: ACTS 2:25–33

Focus verse: *"Seeing what was to come, he spoke of the resurrection of the Messiah, that he was not abandoned to the realm of the dead, nor did his body see decay."* (Acts 2:31)

After teaching from the prophet Joel, Peter continues addressing the crowd on this first Pentecost. He again cites the words of King David, something he did when he led the group into replacing Judas with Matthias (Days 43 and 44). Peter must really connect with David's writings.

We don't think of David as being a prophet. Instead, we know him as a king who is also a poet, having penned many of the psalms in the Bible. Yet Luke calls David a prophet.

Like other prophets whose pronouncements had both a near-term application and a secondary meaning for future generations, many of David's words also carry a double meaning. Though the obvious understanding is to David's own life and situation, whenever his words veer away from his reality, we know he's writing about the future. Such is the case with today's passage, with Peter quoting from Psalm 16:8–11.

When David talks about him not being abandoned to the realm of the dead and the holy one not seeing decay, it's obvious he's not referring to himself. David died. He was buried. His body remained in the tomb where it decomposed. And his tomb is still there for the people to see. This confirms David is dead.

David, however, refers to the holy one who will come after him. This alludes to Jesus. Though Jesus did die and was for a time buried in a tomb, his body did not decay. God did not abandon him there.

His body didn't stay in his grave. Jesus rose from the dead. Peter and the other disciples, along with Mary Magdalene and many others in their group, can testify that Jesus rose from the dead. They are witnesses of his resurrection.

Resurrected Jesus has now ascended into heaven and sits at God's right hand. There he received from his Father the promised gift of the Holy Spirit, which he poured out on his followers. These are the people speaking in other languages so that everyone can hear about Jesus in their native tongue.

Questions: *What can we do to help people hear about Jesus in their own language? How can we tell those around us about Jesus?*

Prayer: Jesus, whether it's near or far away, give us opportunities to tell others about you.

DAY 49: THE PEOPLE RESPOND

TODAY'S PASSAGE: ACTS 2:34–41

Focus verse: *Peter replied, "Repent and be baptized, every one of you, in the name of Jesus Christ for the forgiveness of your sins. And you will receive the gift of the Holy Spirit."* (Acts 2:38)

As Peter continues his message to the people, he shares yet another passage from one of David's psalms (Acts 2:34–35), the fourth time he has done so.

Jesus also quoted this verse (Matthew 22:44, Mark 12:36, and Luke 20:42–43), and it first appeared in Psalm 110:1. This means the passage appears five times in the Bible.

Yet despite its frequent mentions, the verse has also perplexed me. This is because the passage repeats the word *Lord*. Yes, the first says *the* LORD, and the second says *my* Lord, implying a distinction. The dictionary says *Lord* can mean either God or Jesus.

Those who know Hebrew tell me two different Hebrew words appear in this passage, with them both translated as *Lord*. Therefore, the source of my confusion is not the holy text but the English language. Given this, the Amplified Bible reads, "The LORD (Father) says to my Lord (the Messiah, His Son) . . ."

Peter quotes this passage to let the people know that the crucified (and risen) Jesus is both Lord and Messiah.

They understand Peter's teaching. Luke writes "they were cut to the heart." This means they were greatly troubled, terribly upset, and under deep conviction.

Their imperative question to Peter is, "What should we do?"

Peter's answer to them—and to us—is clear: "Repent and be baptized in the name of Jesus for the forgiveness of your sins." It's that easy.

Then Peter gives them a promise. "Afterward you'll receive the gift of the Holy Spirit. This applies to you, your children, and all who are far off."

This last phrase means non-Jews, that is, Gentiles. And they'll receive the Holy Spirit, just like Peter and Jesus's other followers.

Peter continues to teach them. He implores them to follow Jesus. About three thousand people respond. They believe and are baptized.

Three thousand people decide to follow Jesus, but how many in the crowd hear Peter's message but don't respond? Through their lack of action, they reject Jesus.

Three thousand people say yes to Jesus. What an astounding response to Peter's first sermon. Remember that Peter isn't a trained speaker, and his education is minimal. Clearly this is something he couldn't do on his own. But that's what can happen when the Holy Spirit gets involved.

Their group of 120 has grown by three thousand.

And this is just the beginning.

Questions: *What might we accomplish through the Holy Spirit? What can we learn from this first Pentecost to apply to our lives today?*

Prayer: Holy Spirit, thank you for such an amazing response to Peter's message. Show us how you can help us grow Jesus's church today.

DAY 50: THE RESULT OF PENTECOST

TODAY'S PASSAGE: ACTS 2:42–47

Focus verse: *And the Lord added to their number daily those who were being saved.* (Acts 2:47)

What an amazing day Pentecost was. Luke now shares what happens because of what the Holy Spirit did on that day.

This group of over three thousand believers devote themselves to four things.

The first is to the apostles' teaching. Remember these are all Jewish converts to Christianity. They know Judaism, but they're just learning about Jesus. Think of the apostles' teaching as a new member's class.

The second thing they devote themselves to is fellowship. They spend time together with other believers.

Third is to breaking bread. This could be sharing a common meal or a reference to Holy Communion. As Jews, they're most familiar with Passover, and they can now experience Communion as Jesus's extension of the Passover meal.

The fourth thing they devote themselves to is prayer. This is what the disciples did as they waited in Jerusalem for the Holy Spirit to arrive as Jesus promised (Day 42).

As a result, other things happen too.

The apostles perform many wonders and signs, which fills the people with awe. The disciples' first experience in doing this was when Jesus sent them out to the people in groups of two (Mark 6:7–13). Now, under the power of the Holy Spirit, they continue to perform even more miracles.

The believers share everything they have with each other. They even sell property to provide for those in need.

They meet in the temple courts and share meals in people's homes. And they do this with gladness and sincerity, praising God and enjoying the favor of the people.

Because of all this, the Lord continues to grow their numbers. More people are saved every day.

Many look to this passage as an ideal model for the church to follow. And we're wise to consider how we can apply the reality of the early church of Jesus to what we do now. In doing so, however, we must not treat this as a command to follow, but as a description of what happened for us to learn from.

May we discern with wisdom how to proceed.

Questions: *How can we let the experience of the early church inform what we do today? What should we do that we're not presently doing?*

Prayer: Holy Spirit, inspire us through the experiences of the early church to inform what we do now. May the kingdom of God grow as a result.

If you liked *The Victory of Jesus*, please leave a review

online. Your review will help others discover this book and encourage them to read it too.

Thank you.

BOOKS IN THE HOLIDAY CELEBRATION DEVOTIONALS SERIES

Which devotional do you want to read next?

- The Advent of Jesus
- The Passion of Jesus (Lent)
- The Ministry of Jesus
- Thanksgiving with Jesus
- New Year with Jesus

IF YOU'RE NEW TO THE BIBLE

Each entry in this book contains Bible references. These can guide you if you want to learn more. If you're not familiar with the Bible, here's an overview to get you started, give some context, and minimize confusion.

First, the Bible is a collection of works written by various authors over several centuries. Think of the Bible as a diverse anthology of godly communication. It contains historical accounts, poetry, songs, letters of instruction and encouragement, messages from God sent through his representatives, and prophecies.

Most versions of the Bible have sixty-six books grouped into two sections: The Old Testament and the New Testament. The Old Testament contains thirty-nine books that precede and anticipate Jesus. The New Testament includes twenty-seven books and covers Jesus's life and the work of his followers.

The reference notations in the Bible, such as Romans 3:23, are analogous to line numbers in a Shakespearean play. They serve as a study aid. Since the Bible is much longer and more complex than a play, its reference notations are more involved.

As already mentioned, the Bible is an amalgam of books, or sections, such as Genesis, Matthew, or Acts. These are the names given to them, over time, based on the piece's author, audience, or purpose.

In the 1200s, each book was divided into chapters, such as Acts 2 or Psalm 23. In the 1500s, the chapters were further subdivided into verses, such as John 3:16. Let's use this as an example.

The name of the book (John) appears first, followed by the chapter number (3), a colon, and then the verse number (16). Sometimes called a chapter-verse reference notation, this helps people quickly find a specific text regardless of their version of the Bible.

Although the goal was to place these chapter and verse divisions at logical breaks, they sometimes seem arbitrary. Therefore, it's good practice to read what precedes and follows each passage you're studying. The text before or after it may contain relevant insights into the portion you're exploring.

Here's how to look up a specific passage in the Bible based on its reference: Most Bibles contain a table of contents, which gives the page number for the beginning of each book. Start there. Locate the book you want to read, and turn to that page. Then flip forward to the chapter you want. Last, skim that chapter to locate the specific verse.

If you want to read online, enter the reference into BibleGateway.com or BibleHub.com. Also check out the YouVersion app.

Learn more about the greatest book ever written at ABibleADay.com, which provides a Bible blog, summaries of the books of the Bible, a dictionary of Bible terms, Bible reading plans, and other resources.

ABOUT PETER DEHAAN

Peter DeHaan, PhD, wants to change the world one word at a time. His books and blog posts discuss God, the Bible, and church, geared toward spiritual seekers and church dropouts. Many people feel church has let them down, and Peter seeks to encourage them as they search for a place to belong.

But he's not afraid to ask tough questions or make religious people squirm. He's not trying to be provocative. Instead, he seeks truth, even if it makes people uncomfortable. Peter urges Christians to push past the status quo and reexamine how they practice their faith in every part of their lives.

Peter earned his doctorate, awarded with high distinction, from Trinity College of the Bible and Theological Seminary. He lives with his wife in beautiful Southwest Michigan and wrangles crossword puzzles in his spare time.

A lifelong student of Scripture, Peter wrote the 1,000-page website ABibleADay.com to encourage people to explore the Bible, the greatest book ever written. His popular blog addresses biblical Christianity to build a faith that matters.

Read his blog, receive his newsletter, and learn more at PeterDeHaan.com.

BOOKS BY PETER DEHAAN

Holiday Celebration Devotionals

The Advent of Jesus

The Passion of Jesus (Lent)

The Victory of Jesus (Easter)

The Ministry of Jesus

Thanksgiving with Jesus

New Year with Jesus

40-Day Bible Study Series

Dear Theophilus (the Gospel of Luke)

Acts Bible Study

Isaiah Bible Study

Minor Prophets Bible Study

Job Bible Study

Living Water (John)

Love Is Patient (1 and 2 Corinthians)

Revelation Bible Study

1, 2, & 3 John Bible Study

Hebrews Bible Study

James and Jude Bible Study

Matthew Bible Study

1 & 2 Peter Bible Study

Mark Bible Study

Bible Character Sketches Series

Women of the Bible

The Friends and Foes of Jesus

Old Testament Sinners and Saints

More Old Testament Sinners and Saints

Heroes and Heavies of the Apocrypha

200 Old Testament Sinners and Saints

Visiting Churches Series

52 Churches

The 52 Churches Workbook

More Than 52 Churches

The More Than 52 Churches Workbook

Visiting Online Church

Other Books

Elephant God

Jesus's Broken Church

Martin Luther's 95 Theses (formerly *95 Tweets*)

The Christian Church's LGBTQ Failure

Bridging the Sacred-Secular Divide (formerly *Woodpecker Wars*)

Beyond Psalm 150

How Big Is Your Tent?

For the latest list of all Peter's books, go to PeterDeHaan.com/books.

www.ingramcontent.com/pod-product-compliance
Lightning Source LLC
Chambersburg PA
CBHW060918120626
46553CB00001B/372